MY MORNING JACKET

RECORDED VERSIONS GUITAR

AUTHENTIC TRANSCRIPTIONS WITH NOTES AND TABLATURE

Music transcriptions by David Stocker

ISBN 978-1-4234-8294-9

HAL•LEONARD®
CORPORATION
7777 W. BLUEMOUND RD. P.O. BOX 13819 MILWAUKEE, WI 53213

Visit Hal Leonard Online at
www.halleonard.com

from *At Dawn*

Bermuda Highway

Words and Music by Jim James

Capo I

Intro
Fast ♩ = 157

*Symbols in parentheses represent chord names respective to capoed guitar. Symbols above represent actual sounding chords.
Capoed fret is "0" in tab. Chord symbols reflect overall harmony.

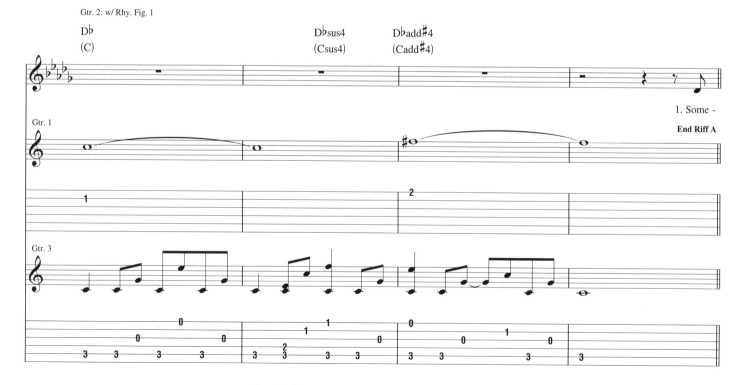

Verse

Gtr. 1 tacet

Db
(C)

Fm
(Em)

times I walk a-round town look-in' at fac - es, __ won-d'rin' why their bod-ies go to sil - ly plac - es. __

Gtr. 3

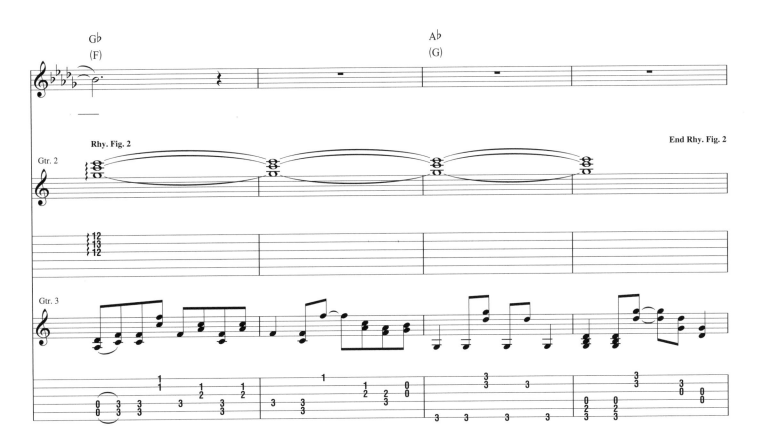

Gb
(F)

Ab
(G)

Rhy. Fig. 2

End Rhy. Fig. 2

Gtr. 2

Gtr. 3

Gtr. 2: w/ Rhy. Fig. 2 (2 times)

Db
(C)

Fm
(Em)

Walk-in' past car-pet mills, look-in' in and tak-in' stills. Your ass, it draws __ me in __ like a Ber-mu-da

Gtr. 3

*T = Thumb on 6th string

4

Gtr. 2: w/ Rhy. Fig. 1

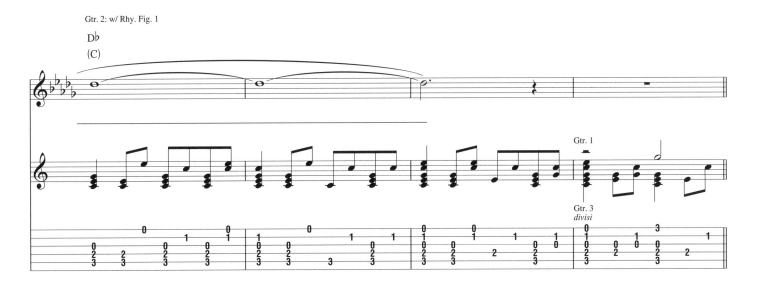

Interlude
Gtr. 1: w/ Riff A
Gtr. 2: w/ Rhy. Fig. 1 (2 times)

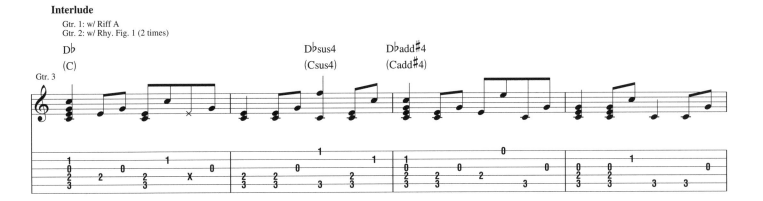

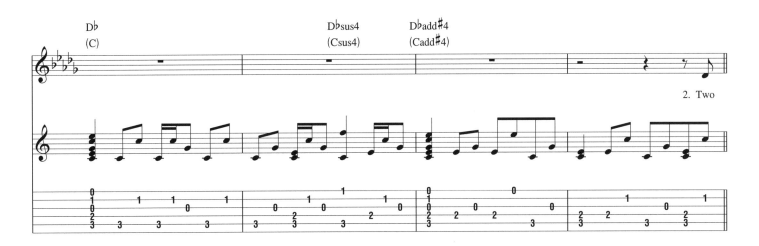

2. Two

Verse

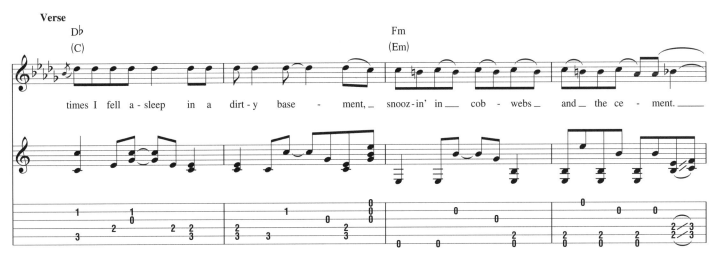

times I fell a-sleep in a dirt-y base - ment, snooz-in' in __ cob - webs __ and __ the ce - ment. __

Db
(C)

Interlude

Gtr. 2: w/ Rhy. Fig. 1

Dbadd#4   Dbsus4   Db
(Cadd#4)   (Csus4)   (C)

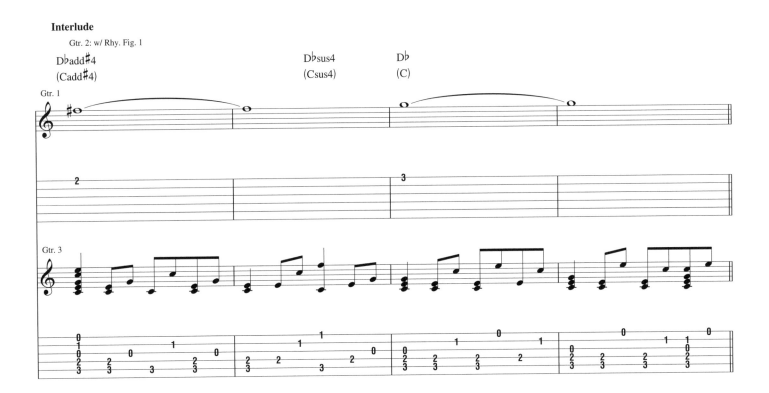

Chorus

Gtr. 1 tacet

Fm   Gb
(Em)   (F)

Oh,   don't carve me   out. _____   Don't let your _

sil - ly dreams _____ fall in be - tween _____

crack of the bed _____ and the wall. _____ Ah. _____

Gtr. 2: w/ Rhy. Fig. 2

Oh, don't carve me out. _____ Don't let your

8

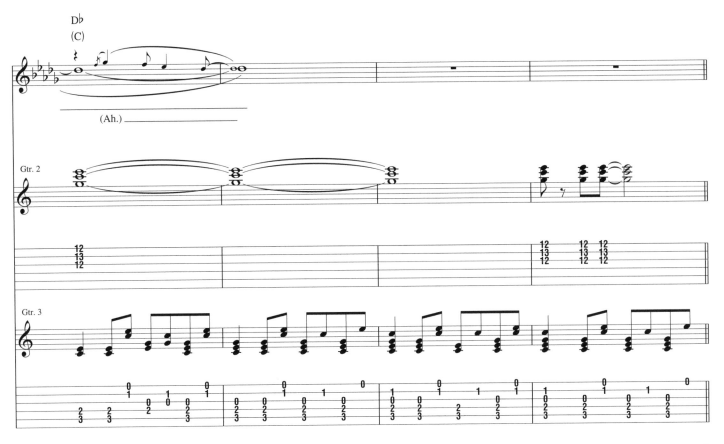

Outro

Gtr. 2: w/ Rhy. Fig. 1 (3 times)

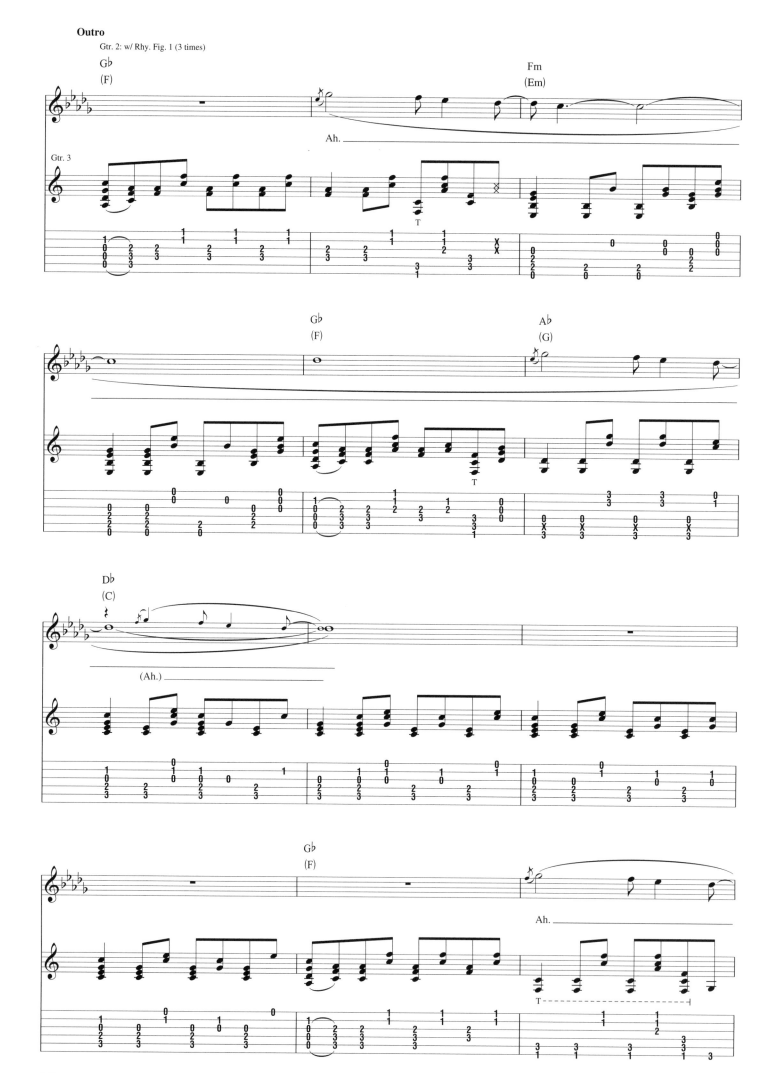

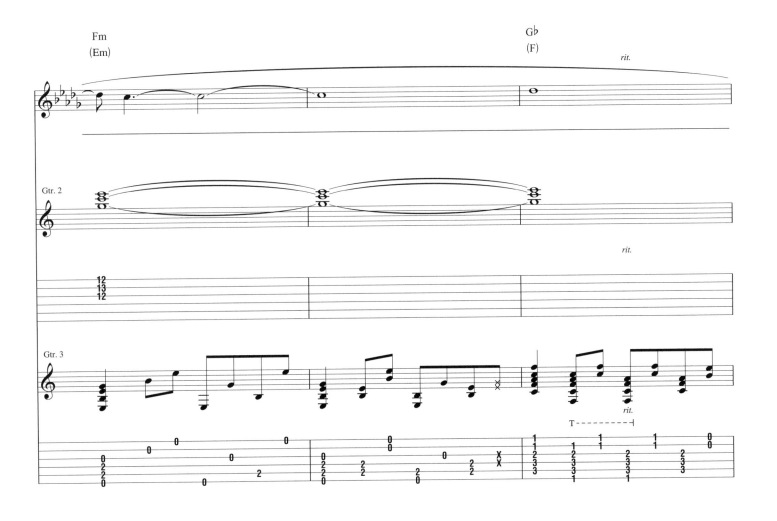

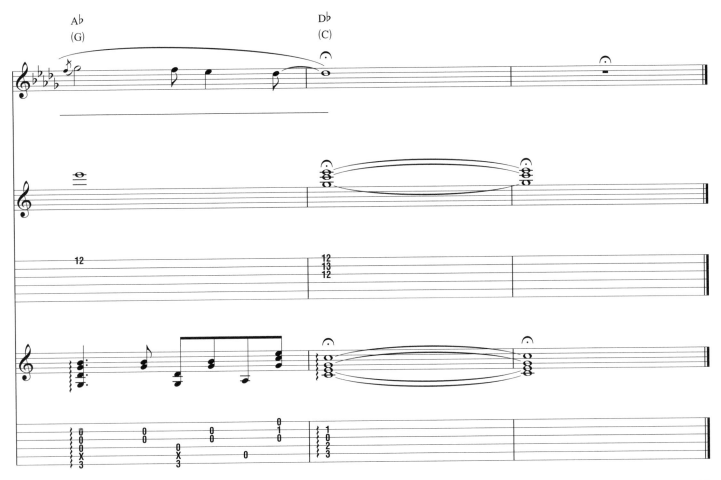

from *Z*

Dondante

Words and Music by Jim James

Gtr. 1: Capo III

*Symbols in parentheses represent chord names respective to capoed guitar. Symbols above represent actual sounding chords.
Capoed fret is "0" in tab. Chord symbols reflect overall harmony.

Verse

Gtr. 1 tacet

2. And all ___ that ev-er mat-tered will some-day ___ turn back to bat-ter like ___ a ___

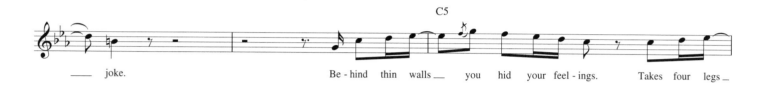

___ joke. Be-hind thin walls ___ you hid your feel-ings. Takes four legs ___

___ to make a ceil-ing, like ___ a ___ thing. In a dream ___

*P.M.

*While muting strings near the bridge with the palm of your pick hand, rapidly "strum" the strings with the side of your thumb.

___ I saw you walk-in' with your friends ___ a-live ___ and talk-in', that ___ was ___ you.

Guitar Solo

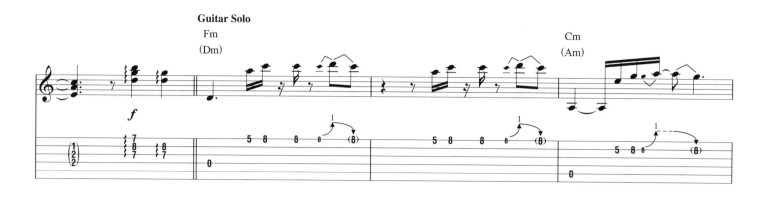

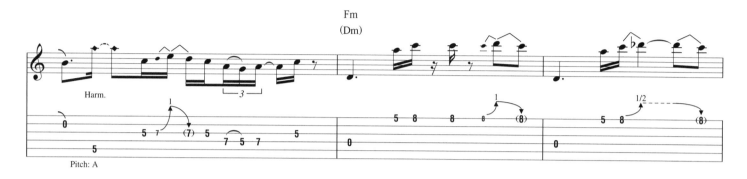

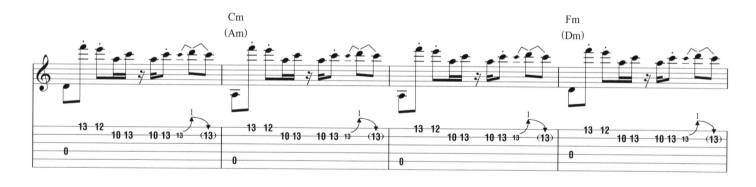

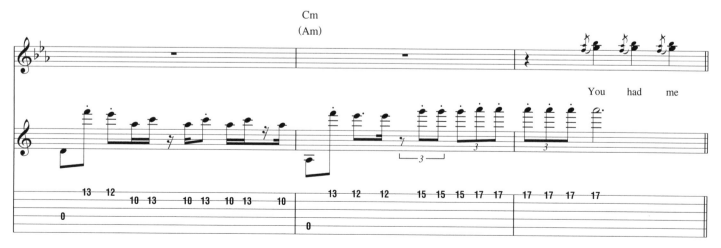

Chorus

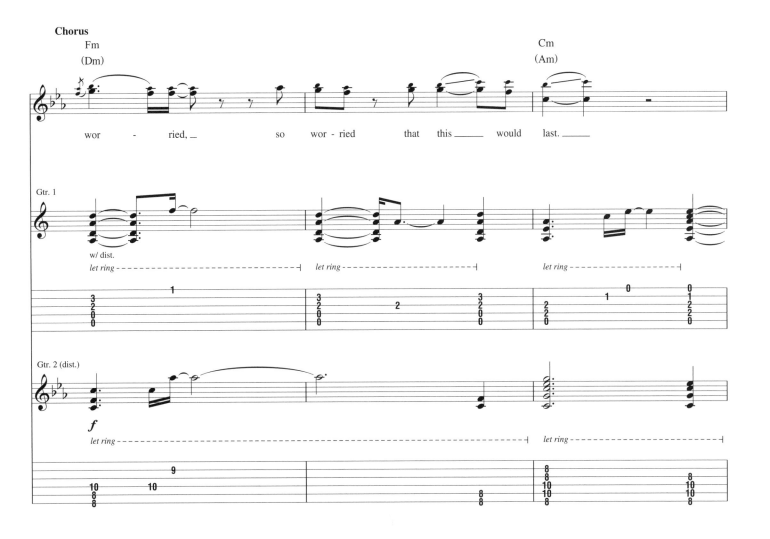

wor - ried, __ so wor - ried that this ___ would last. ___

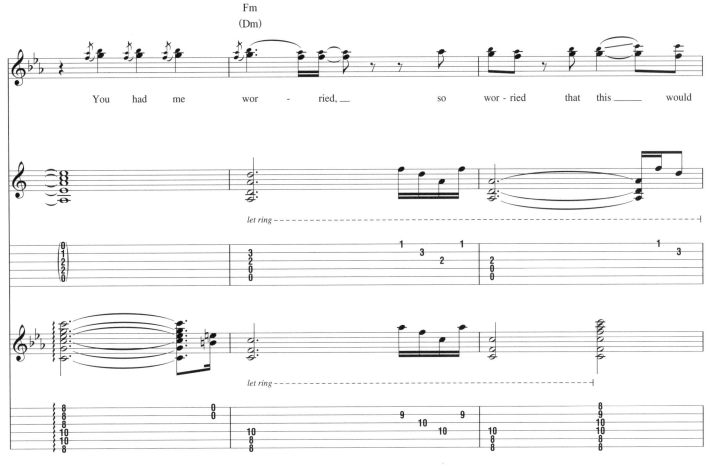

You had me wor - ried, __ so wor - ried that this ___ would

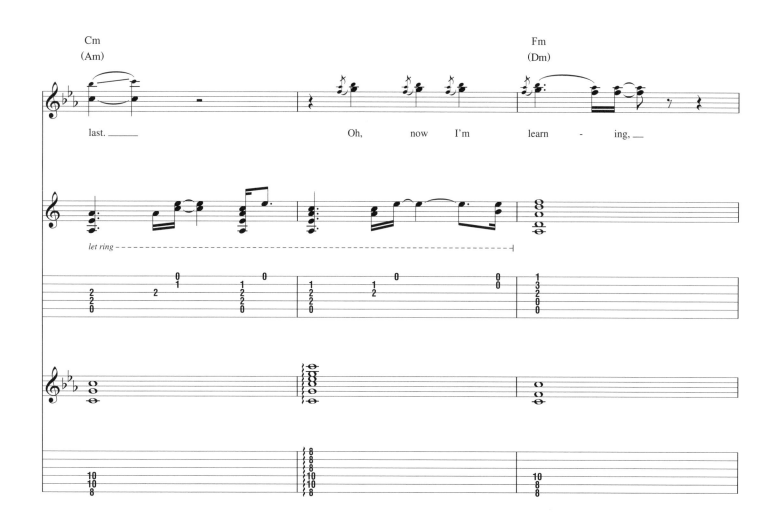

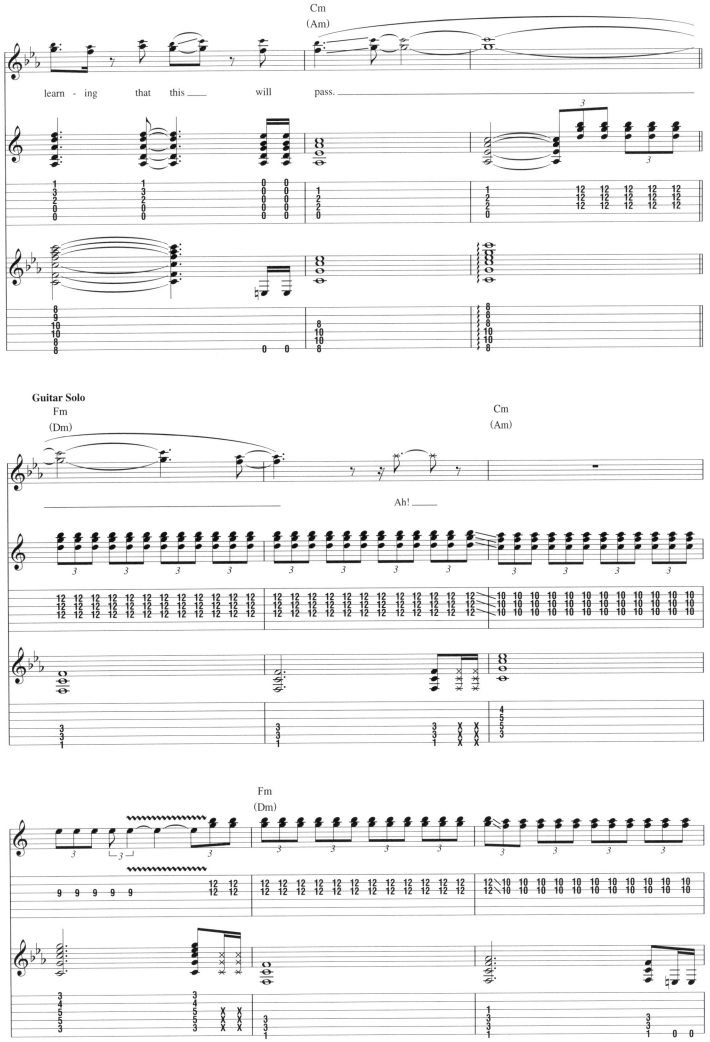

learn - ing   that   this ___   will   pass. _____

Guitar Solo

Ah! ___

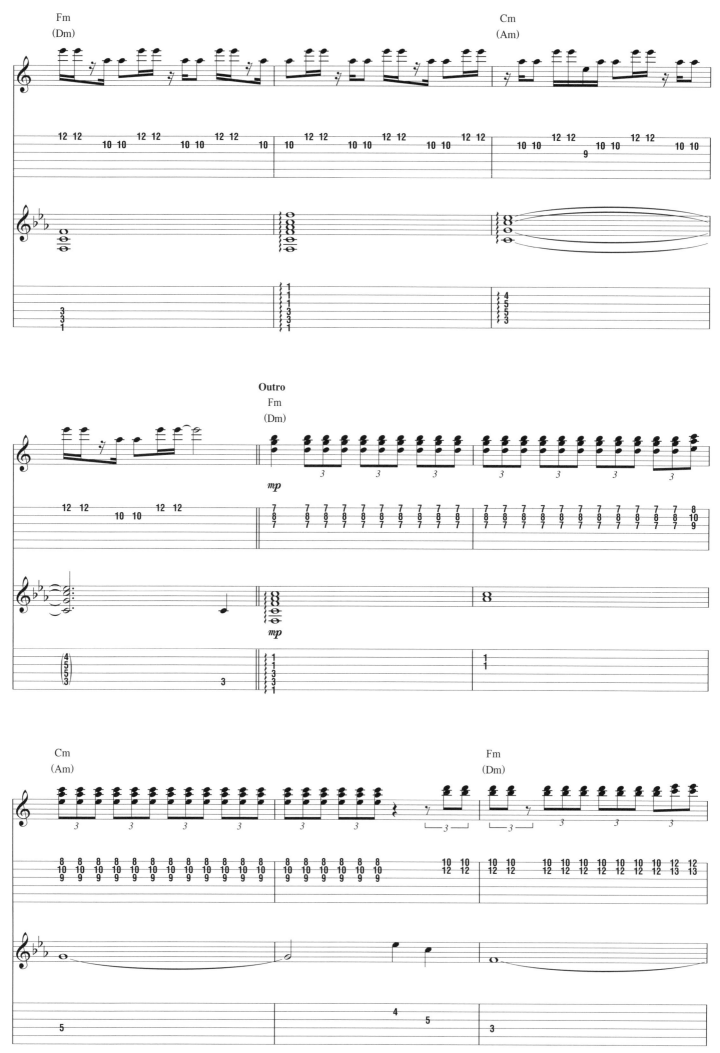

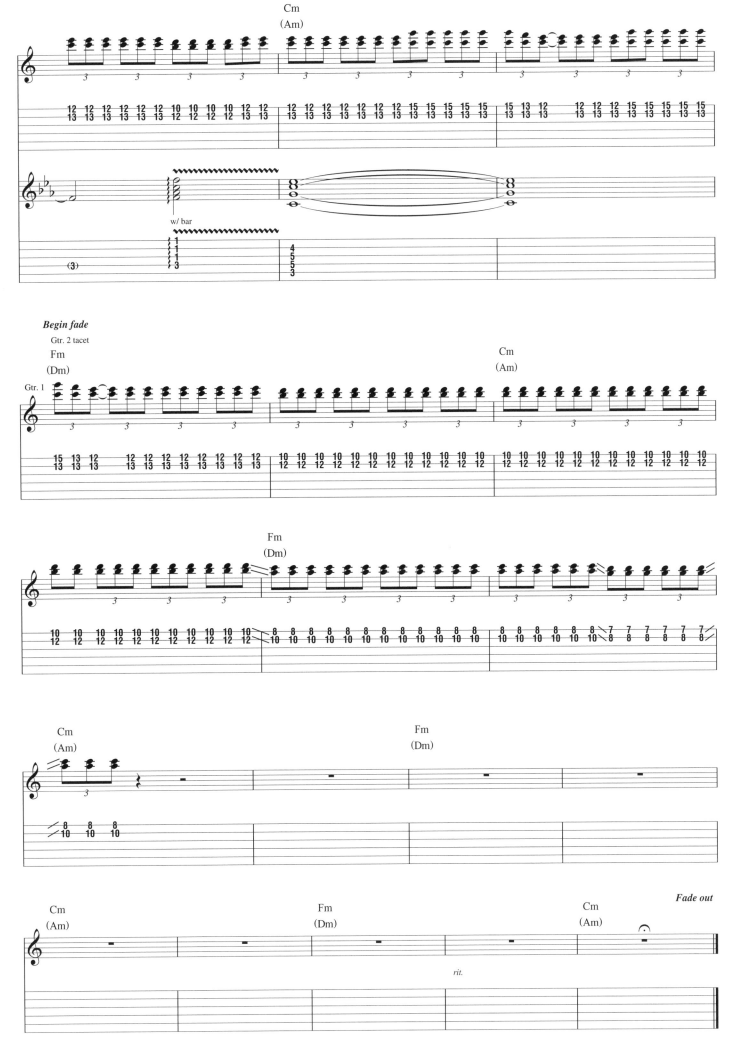

Evil Urges

Words and Music by Jim James

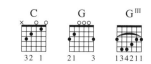

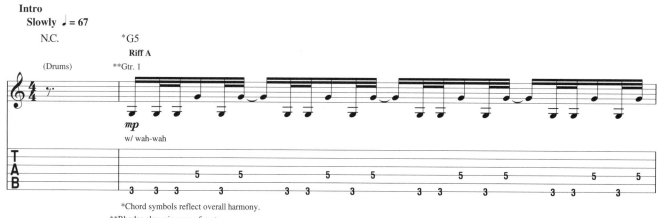

*Chord symbols reflect overall harmony.

**Rhodes elec. piano arr. for gtr.

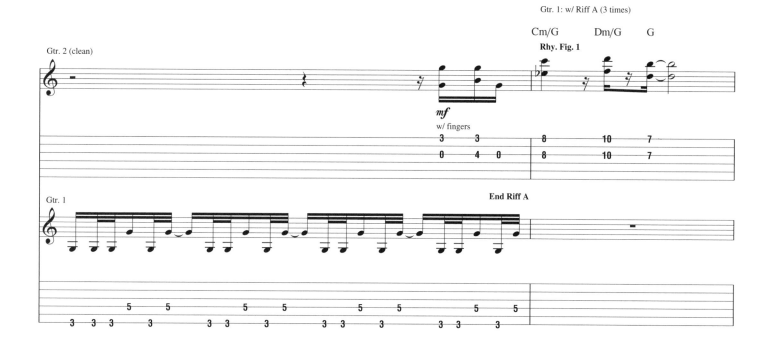

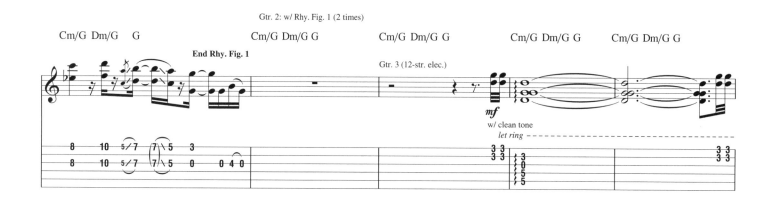

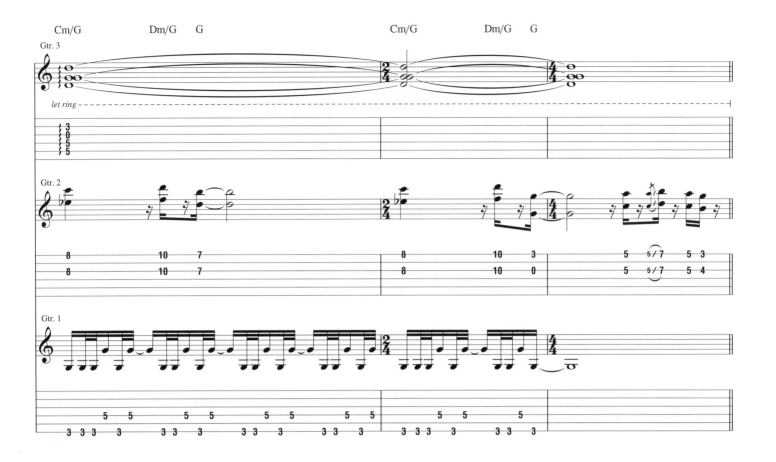

Verse

Gtr. 1 tacet

1. Well, what is ___ what?_ Man, they got us so scared. ___

*Piano arr. for gtr.

Think-in' we're so e - vil way down un - der there.____

Oo, I made a nas - ty de - ci - sion____

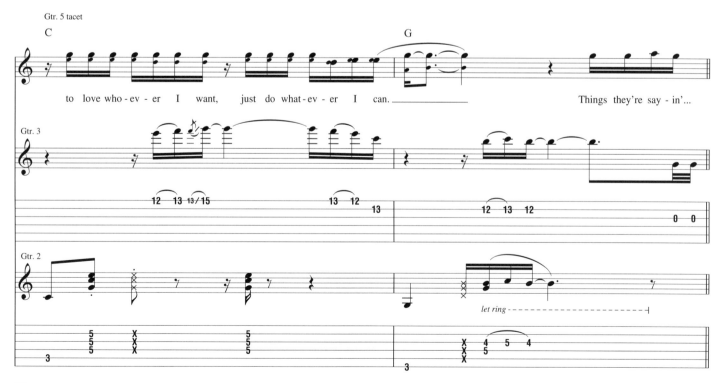

to love who - ev - er I want, just do what - ev - er I can.____ Things they're say - in'...

Chorus

Gtr. 1: w/ Riff A (3 times)
Gtr. 2: w/ Rhy. Fig. 1 (3 times)

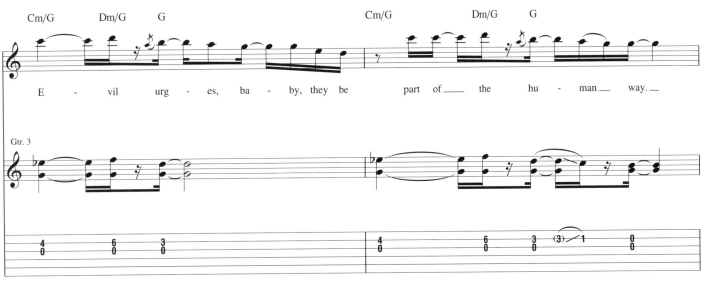

E - vil urg - es, ba - by, they be part of ___ the hu - man __ way. __

Gtr. 3

It ain't e - vil, ba - by, if it ain't hurt - in' an - y - bod - y.

E - vil urg - es, ba - by, they be part of ___ the hu - man __ way. __

It ain't e - vil, ba - by, if it ain't hurt-in' an - y-bod-y, an-y-bod-y.

Verse

Gtr. 1 tacet
Gtr. 4: w/ Riff B1 (2 times)

___ 2. If it's all the same, we're tired of wait - in'. Come on, then, _____

let ring - - - - - - - - - - - - - - -   *let ring - -*

and ded - i - cate___ your love   to   an - y wom-an or man.___

Riff C   End Riff C

Gtr. 5: w/ Riff C

No ra-cial bound - 'ry lines,   no so-cial sub - di - vi - sions.___   If you

Gtr. 3

Gtr. 2

Gtr. 4

Gtr. 4 tacet

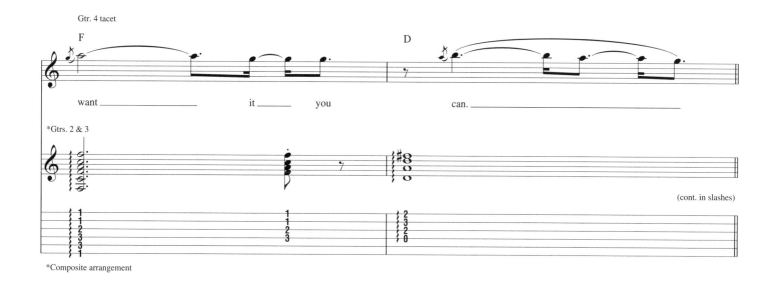

want ____ it ____ you ____ can. ____

*Gtrs. 2 & 3

(cont. in slashes)

*Composite arrangement

Bridge

We're not say - in', I'm not say - in' that I want it some - day. ____

Gtr. 6 (slight dist.)

mp

*w/ octaver

*Set for one octave higher.

Gtrs. 2 & 3: w/ Rhy. Fig. 2 (7 times)

And we're not say - in', I'm not say - in' that I want it some - how. ____

Riff D   **End Riff D**

Gtr. 6: w/ Riff D (5 times)

And we're not say - in', I'm not say - in' that I want it some day, ____ some - how. ____
(Day.) ____

Interlude

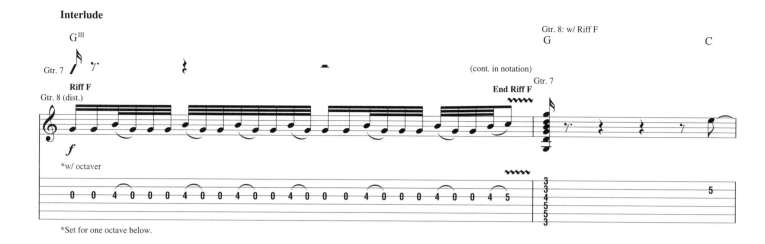

**w/ octaver

*Set for one octave below.

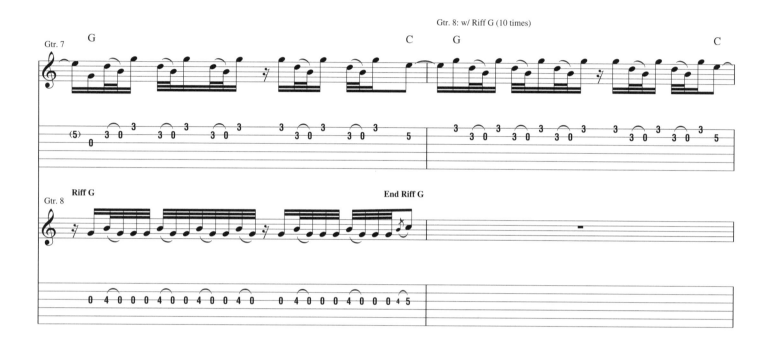

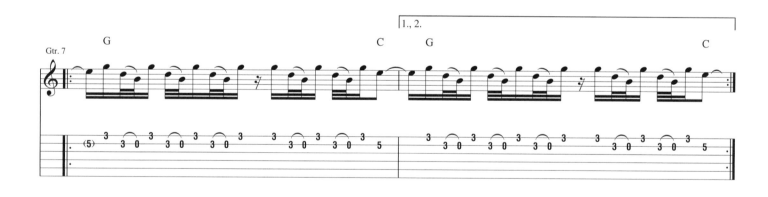

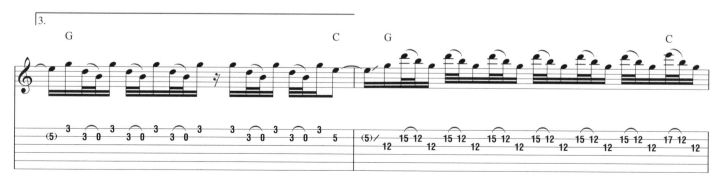

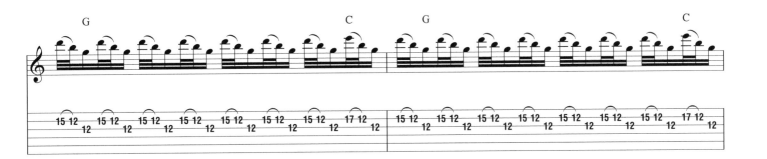

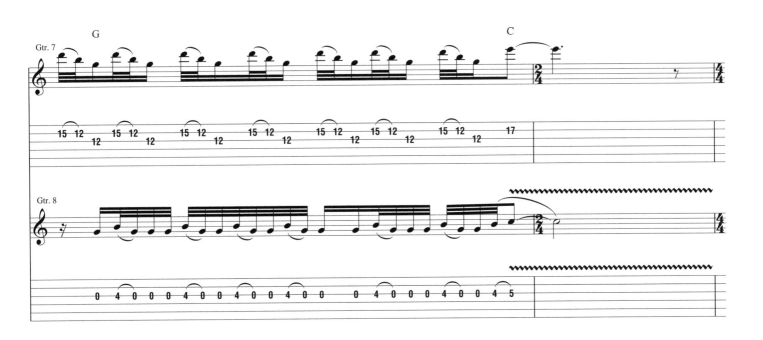

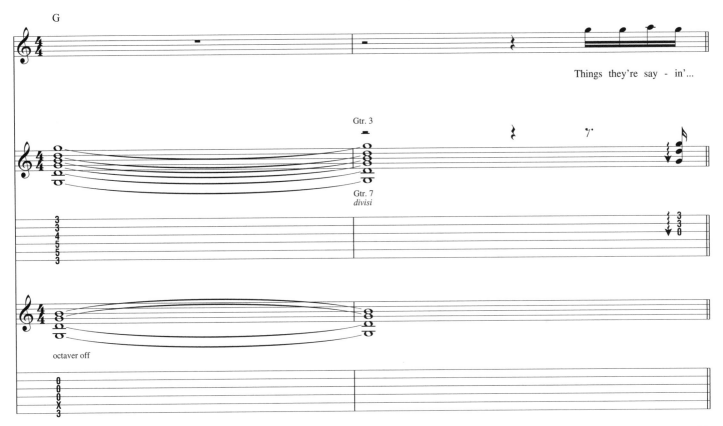

Things they're say - in'...

Outro-Chorus

Gtr. 1: w/ Riff A (7 times)
Gtr. 2: w/ Rhy. Fig. 1 (7 times)
Gtrs. 7 & 8 tacet

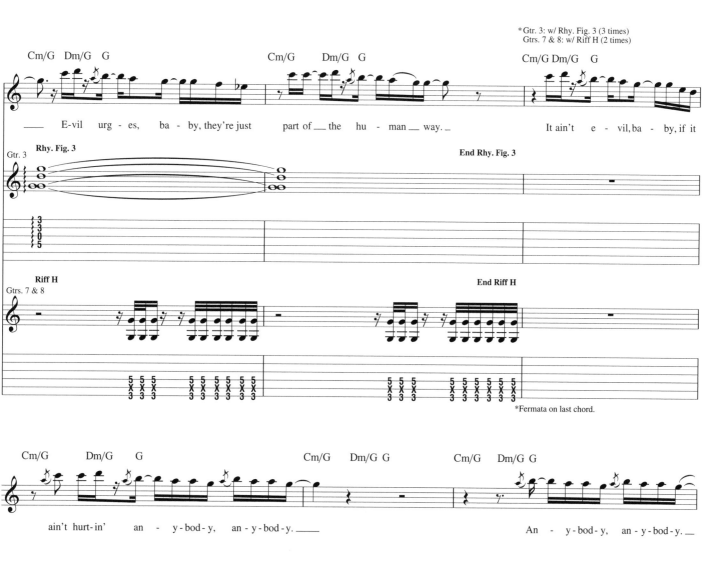

E-vil urg - es, ba - by, they're just part of __ the hu - man __ way. __ It ain't e - vil, ba - by, if it

*Fermata on last chord.

ain't hurt-in' an - y - bod - y, an - y - bod - y. __ An - y - bod - y, an - y - bod - y. __

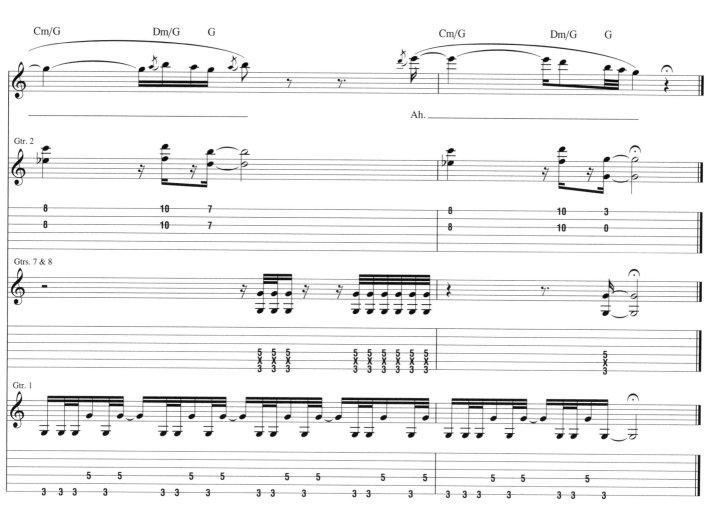

Ah. _____

Gideon

Words and Music by Jim James

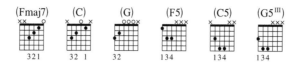

Capo III

Intro
Moderately fast ♩ = 129

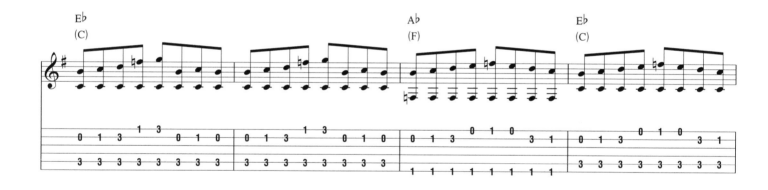

*Symbols in parentheses represent chord names respective to capoed guitar.
Symbols above represent actual sounding chords. Capoed fret is "0" in tab.
Chord symbols reflect basic harmony.

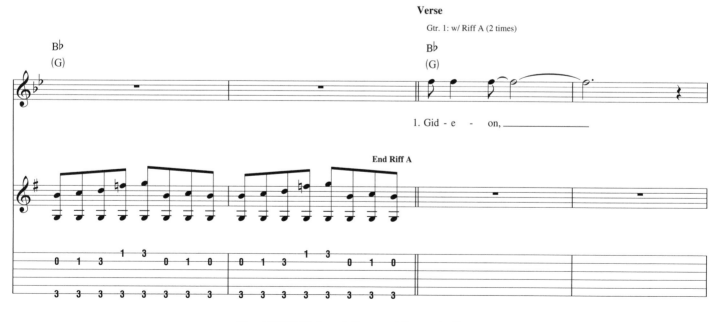

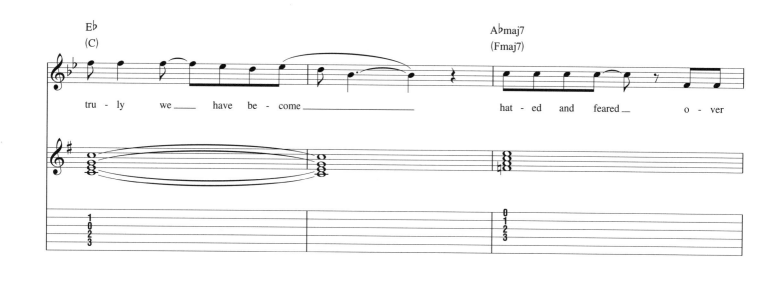

tru - ly we___ have be - come___ hat - ed and feared___ o - ver

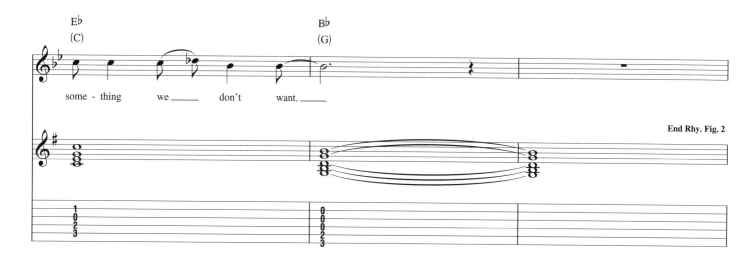

some - thing we___ don't want.___

End Rhy. Fig. 2

Gtr. 2: w/ Rhy. Fig. 2

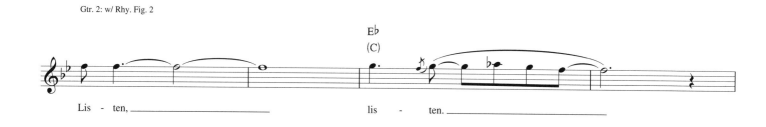

Lis - ten,___ lis - ten.___

Most of us___ be - lieve that this is wrong.___ An - i - mal,___

*Gtr. 3 (dist.)

*Two gtrs. arr. for one.

Outro

**Gtr. 1: w/ Riff A (1st 2 meas., till fade)

**dist. off

Play 6 times and fade

Gtrs. 2, 3 & 4 tacet

from *It Still Moves*

Golden

Words and Music by Jim James

Gtrs. 1 & 4: Open E minor tuning, Capo I:
(low to high) E-B-E-G-B-E

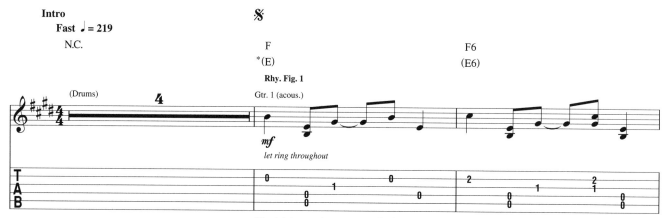

*Symbols in parentheses represent chord names repective to capoed guitar. Symbols above represent
actual sounding chords. Capoed fret is "0" in tab. Chord symbols reflect implied harmony.

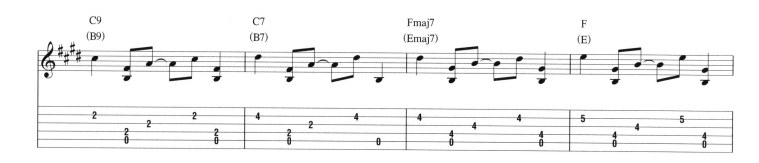

miles of light ex - plode. ___
hot on my ___ skin a - gain. ___

Drift - in' off ___ a thing ___ I've nev -
Feel - in' good, ___ a thing ___ I've ___ nev -

er done be - fore. ___
er known be - fore. ___

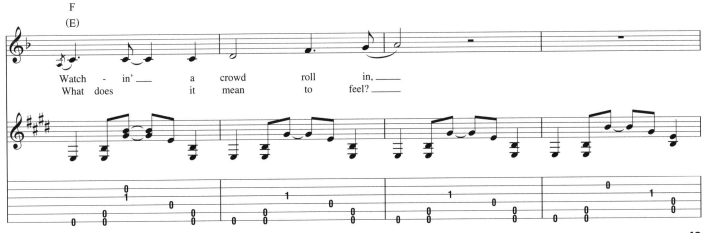

Watch - in' ___ a crowd roll in, ___
What does it mean to feel? ___

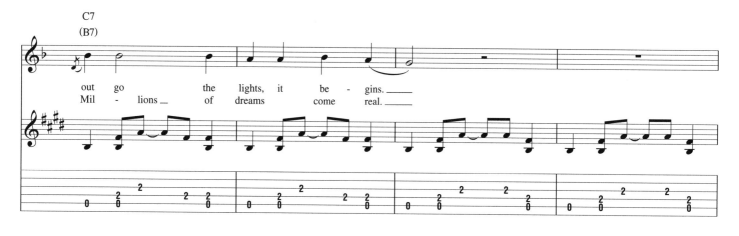

out go the lights, it be - gins. _____
Mil - lions _ of dreams come real. _____

Feel - ing in _____ my bones _____ I've nev -
Feel - ing in _____ my soul _____ I've nev -

To Coda ⊕

2nd time, Gtr. 2: w/ Fill 1

er felt _____ be - fore. _____ }
er felt be - fore. _____ }

Mm. _____

Gtr. 2 (elec.)

mp
w/ slight dist.

Gtr. 1

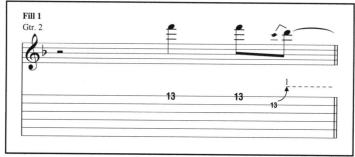

Fill 1
Gtr. 2

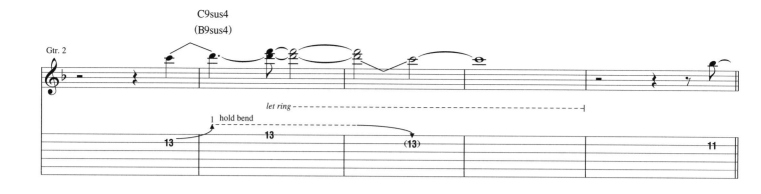

Chorus

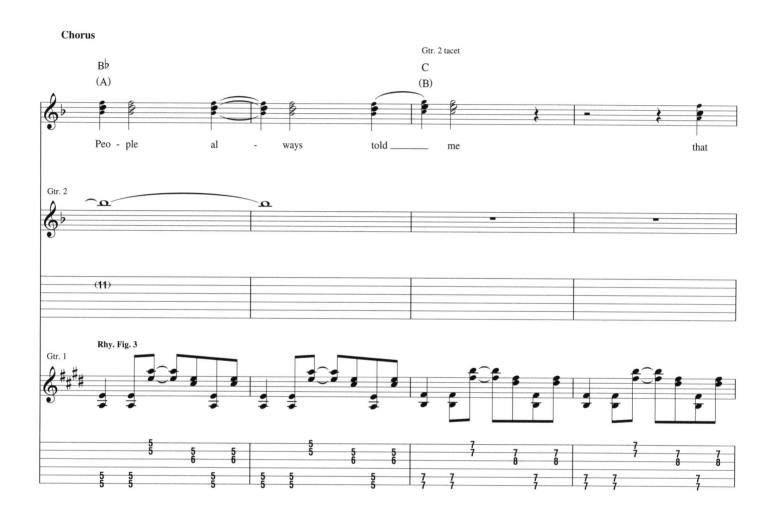

People al - ways told _____ me that

bars are dark and lone - ly, and

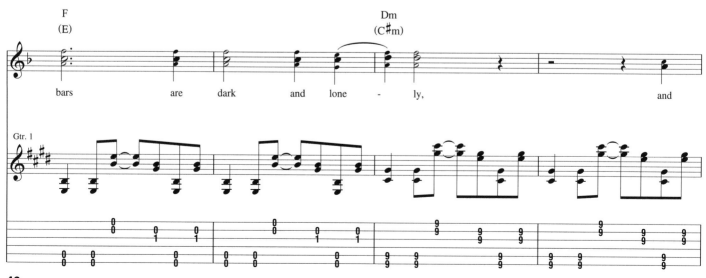

46

talk   is   of - ten   cheap ____   and   filled ____   with   air. ____

End Rhy. Fig. 3

Gtr. 1: w/ Rhy. Fig. 3

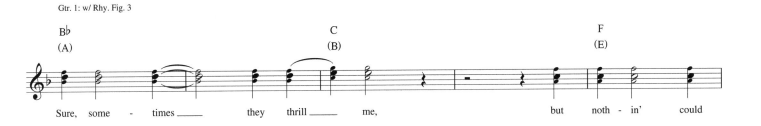

Sure,   some - times ____   they   thrill ____   me,   but   noth - in'   could

ev - er   chill ____   me   like   the   way   they   make   the   time ____

D.S. al Coda

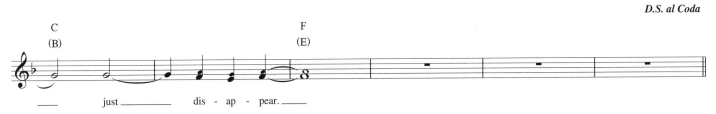

____   just ____   dis - ap - pear. ____

⊕ Coda

Interlude

Gtr. 1: w/ Rhy. Fig. 2 (2 times)

Fmaj7
(Emaj7)

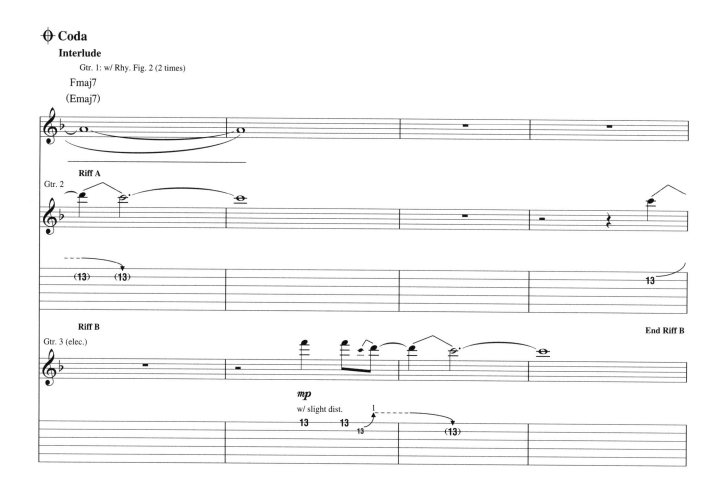

Gtr. 2

Riff A

Riff B

End Riff B

Gtr. 3 (elec.)

mp

w/ slight dist.

C9sus4
(B9sus4)

End Riff A

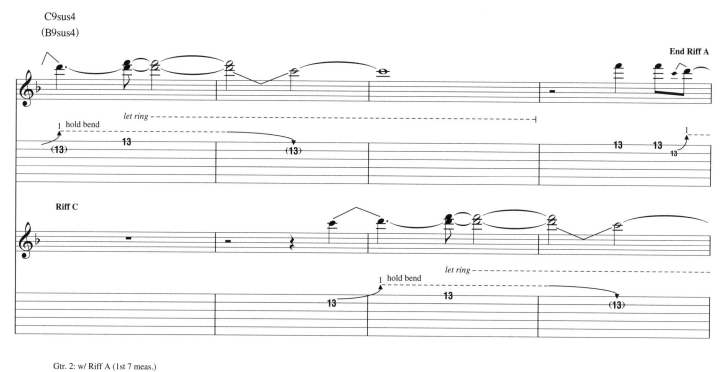

let ring

hold bend

Riff C

let ring

hold bend

Gtr. 2: w/ Riff A (1st 7 meas.)

Fmaj7
(Emaj7)

Gtr. 3

End Riff C

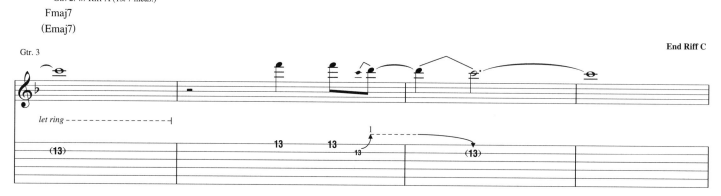

let ring

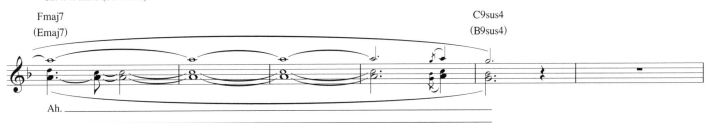

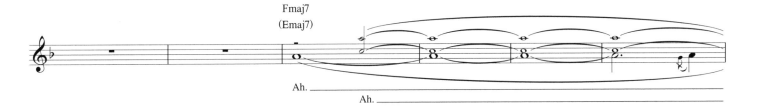

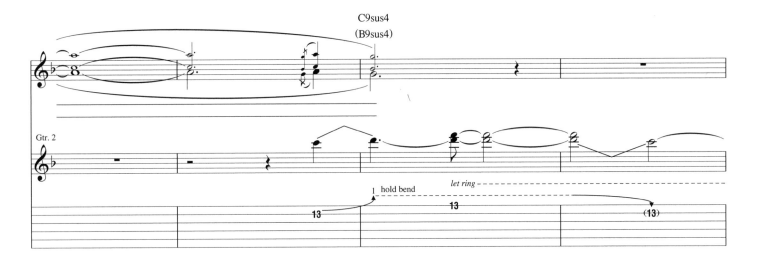

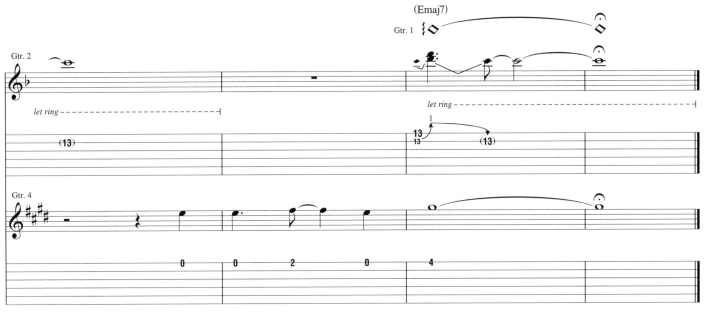

Highly Suspicious

Words and Music by Jim James

*Synth arr. for gtr.

**Symbols in parentheses represent chord names respective to capoed guitar. Symbols above represent actual sounding chords.
Capoed fret is "0" in tab. Chord symbols reflect overall harmony.

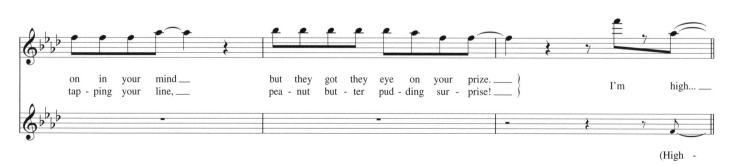

(High -

Chorus

F5
(E5)

high - ly sus-pi-cious of you. I'm high...

- ly sus-pi-cious, high - ly sus-pi-cious of you. High -

Rhy. Fig. 1 **End Rhy. Fig. 1**

Gtrs. 2 & 3 (dist.)

mf

Gtrs. 2 & 3: w/ Rhy. Fig. 1

high - ly sus-pi-cious of you. 2. Now

- ly sus-pi-cious, high - ly sus-pi-cious of you.)

Verse

Fm7add4
(Em7add4)

3. Wast-ing all your time on dra-ma, could be solv-ing real crime. Waste a-way your mind too. I'm high...

††
Gtr. 5

Gtr. 2
divisi
†††

*
Harm.

*Vol. swell

Pitch: D
††Vol. swell
†††Gtr. 5 to left of slash in tab.

Gtr. 3 Gtr. 3

Gtr. 4 (dist.)
divisi
***
Harm.
mf

**
Harm.
mf

Pitch: E
**Vol. swell

***Vol. swell
†Gtr. 3 to left of slash in tab.

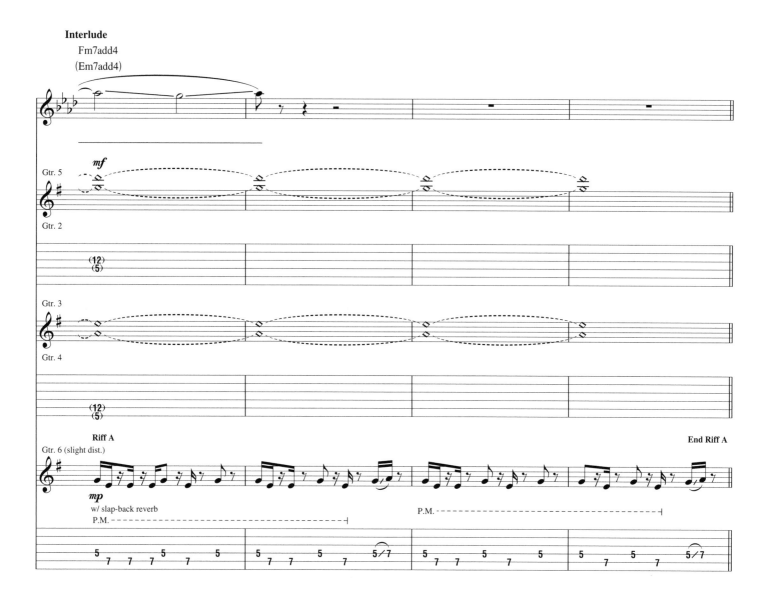

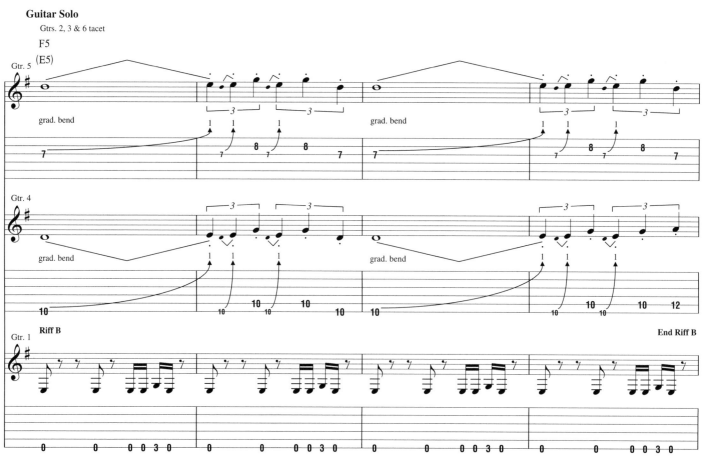

Interlude

Gtr. 6: w/ Riff A

Fm
(Em)

Ah, _____ ah. _____ Ah. _____

(High -

*Gtrs. 2, 3 & 7

*Gtr. 7 (dist.); Composite arrangement

**Vol. swell

pp **   f

Chorus

Gtrs. 2 & 3: w/ Rhy. Fig. 2 (4 times)

F5
(E5)

- ly sus - pi - cious,   high - ly sus - pi - cious of you.   High -

Gtr. 7

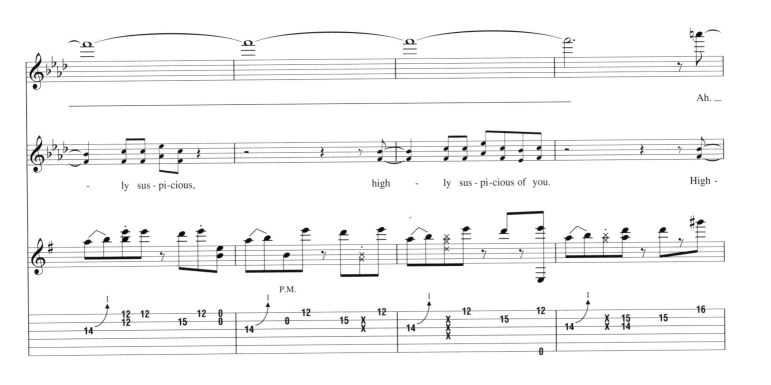

Ah. __

-ly sus-pi-cious, high - ly sus-pi-cious of you. High -

-ly sus - pi - cious, high -

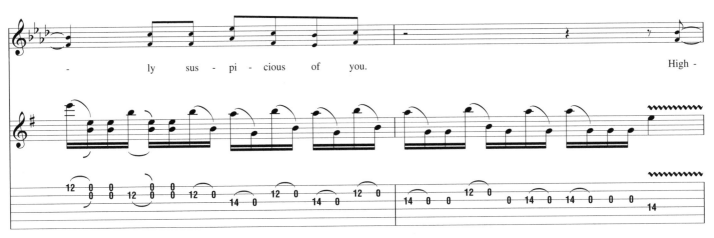

-ly sus - pi - cious of you. High -

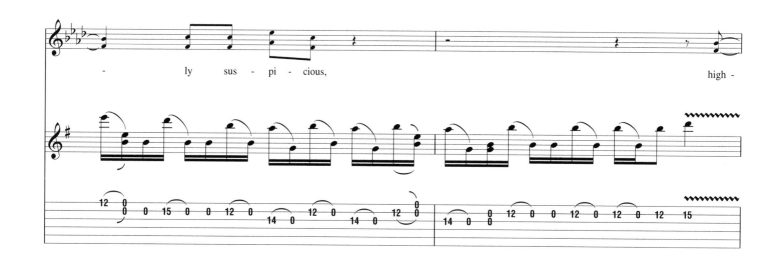

- ly sus - pi - cious,   high -

- ly sus - pi - cious of you.)

Outro

Gtrs. 2 & 3: w/ Rhy. Fig. 1 (1st 3 meas.)

Fm
(Em)

N.C.

Gtr. 7

*fdbk.

Pitch: C#

*Microphonic fdbk., not caused by string vibration.

Gtr. 1

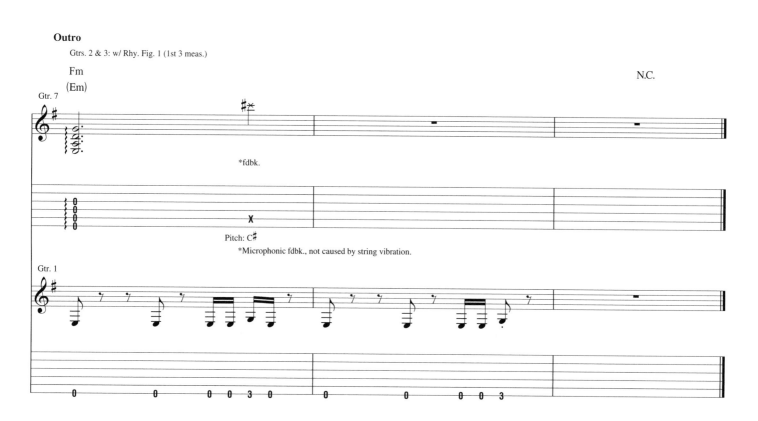

I'm Amazed

Words and Music by Jim James

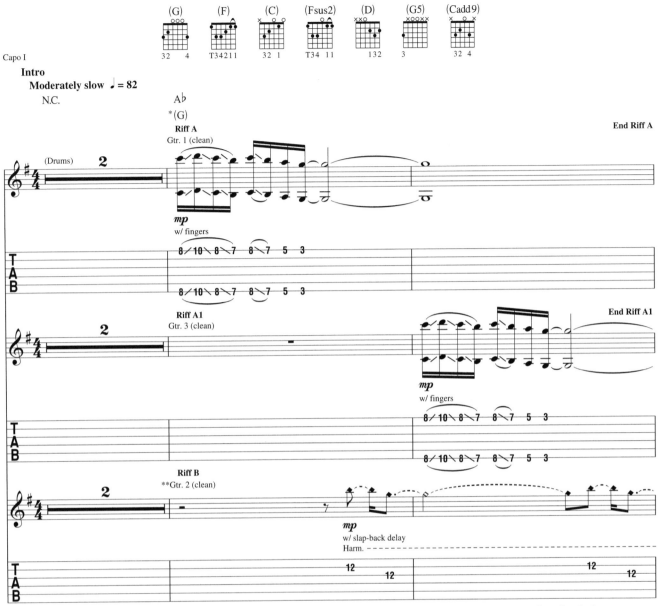

*Symbols in parentheses represent chord names respective to capoed guitar. Symbols above represent actual sounding chords.
Capoed fret is "0" in tab. Chord symbols reflect overall harmony.

**Two gtrs. arr. for one.

Gtr. 6 tacet

(D)

Gtr. 4

(C)

End Voc. Fig. 1

* Voc. Fig. 1

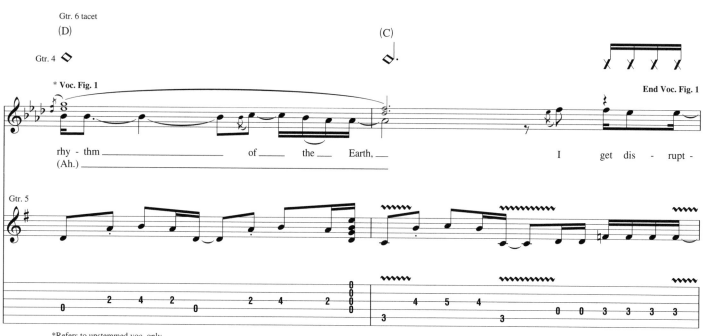

rhy - thm _____ of _____ the ___ Earth, _____   I   get dis - rupt-
(Ah.) _____

Gtr. 5

*Refers to upstemmed voc. only

(G)

(C)

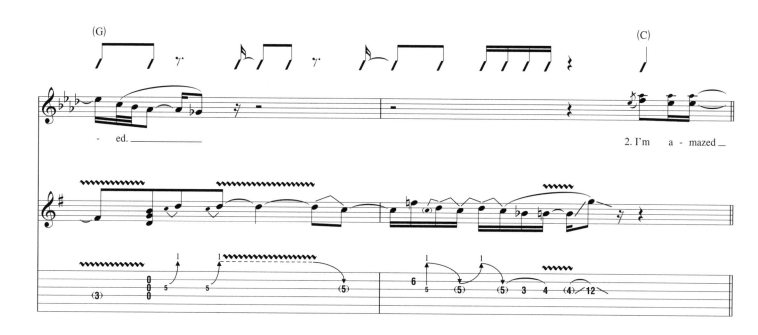

- ed. _____

2. I'm a - mazed __

Verse

Gtr. 4: w/ Rhy. Fig. 1
Gtr. 5 tacet
Gtr. 6: w/ Riff C

A♭
(G)

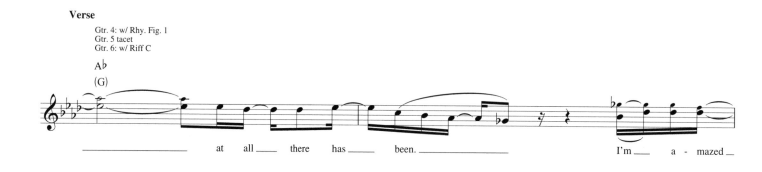

_____   at   all ____ there has _____ been. _____   I'm ___ a - mazed __

D♭   A♭   N.C.   D♭
(C)   (G)   (C)

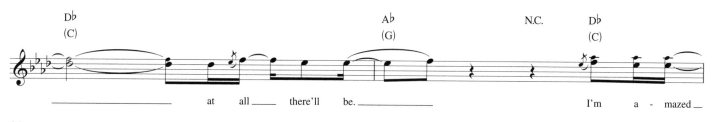

_____   at   all ____ there'll be. _____   I'm a - mazed __

64

Guitar Solo

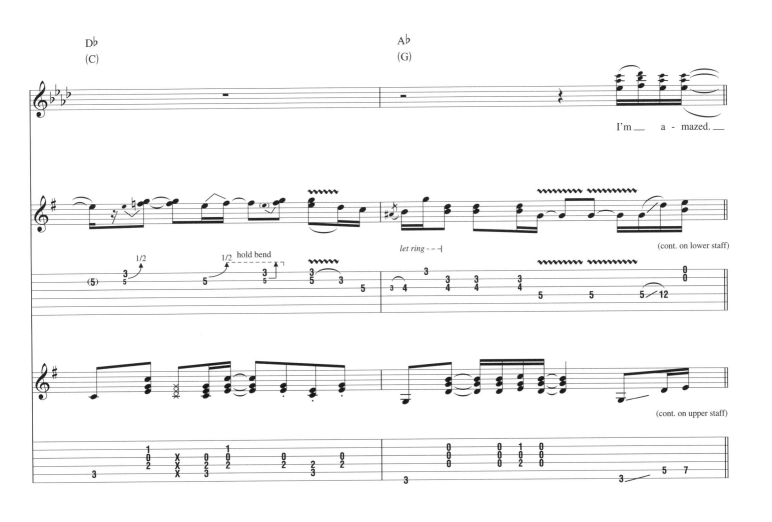

Bridge

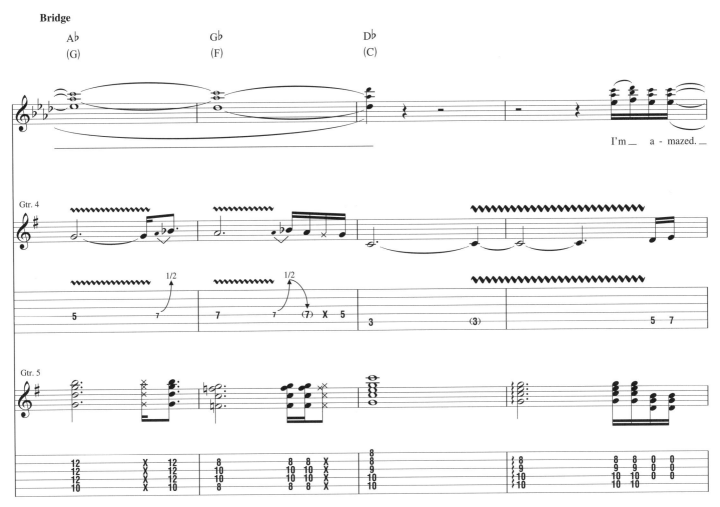

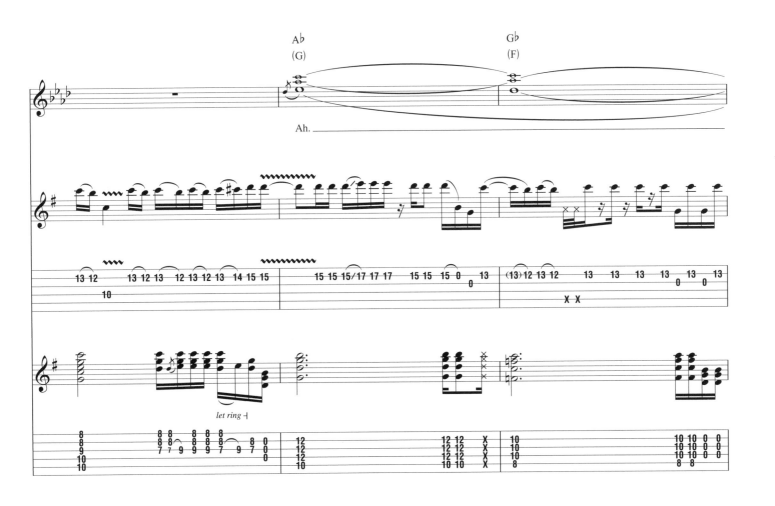

Outro

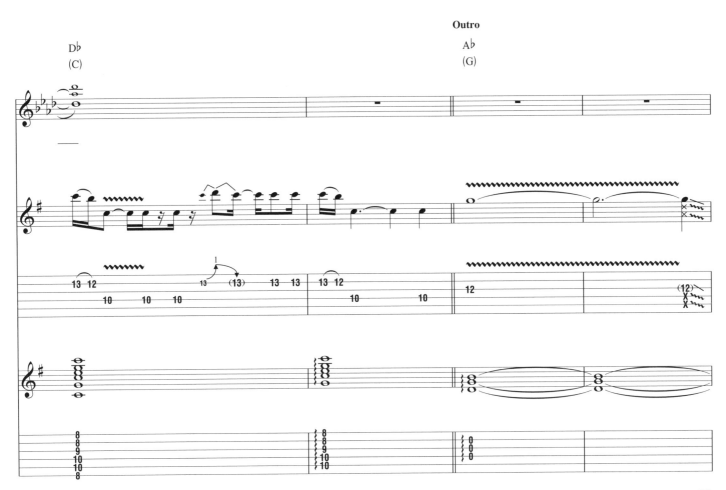

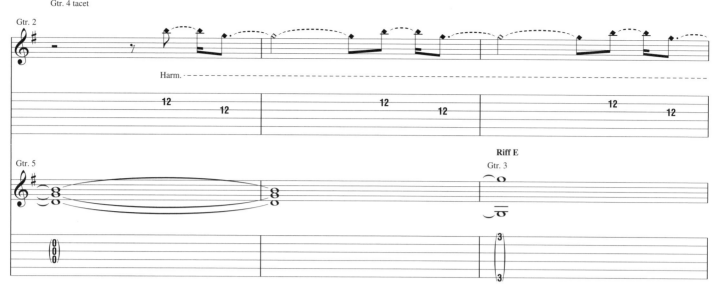

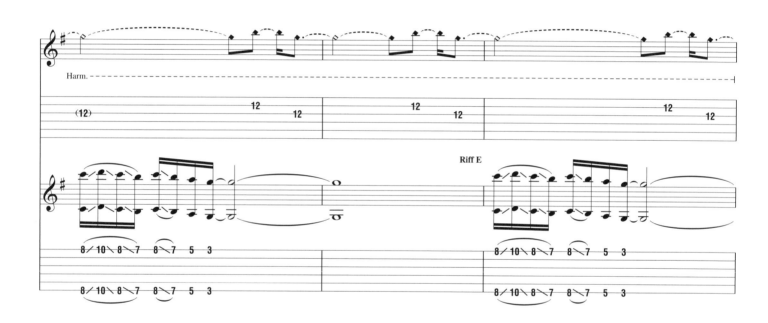

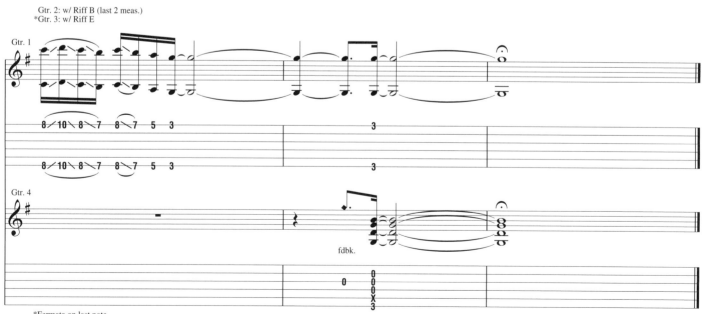

*Fermata on last note.

from *Z*

Lay Low

Words and Music by Jim James

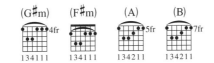

Capo III

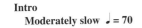

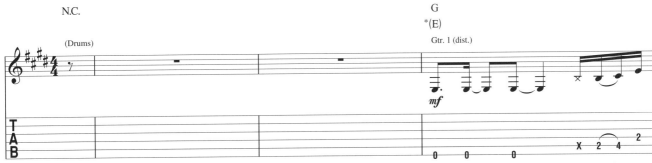

*Symbols in parentheses represent chord names respective to capoed guitar. Symbols above represent actual sounding chords. Capoed fret is "0" in tab. Chord symbols reflect overall harmony.

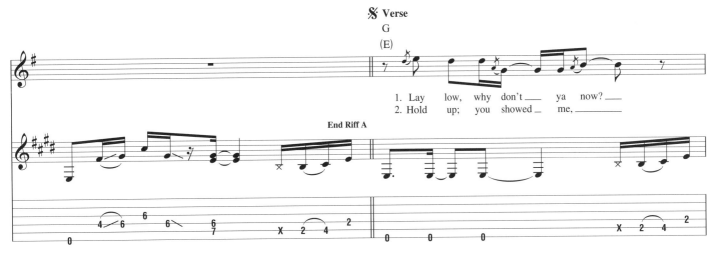

1. Lay low, why don't___ ya now?___
2. Hold up; you showed___ me, _____

Lay back a while ___ and I'll ___ show ya; ___ got the good that you want, no need ___ to go
oh, what you told ___ me. ___ It's not ___ what you want but what you need. ___ It's not a

hunt some-thin' else, it's right ___ here with me ___ when you stay. _____
head full of pills or am - phet - a - mines ___ when you stay. _____

It's al - ways good when I get to see ___ that there's

nev - er more than what you're tell - in' me ___ when you stay ___ home.

(A)

Am
(F#m)

D
(B)

G
(E)

C
(A)

Am
(F#m)

D
(B)

G
(E)

let ring

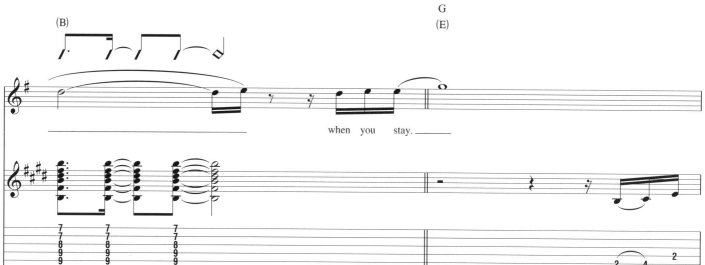

D.S. al Coda

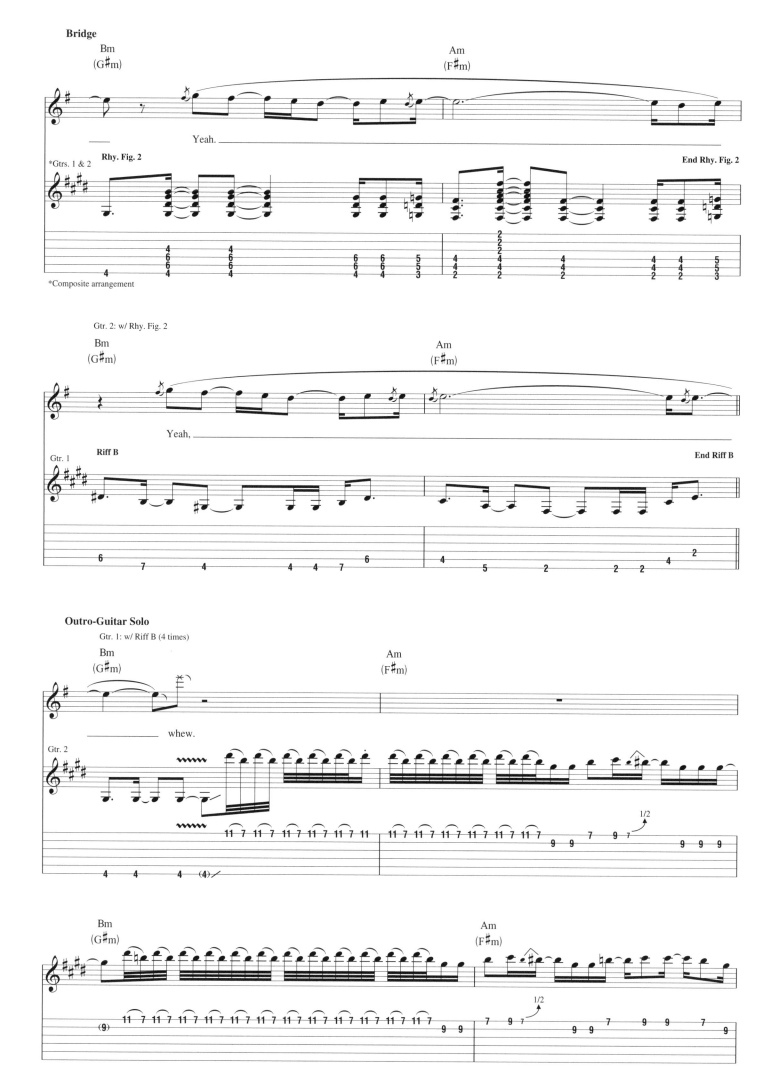

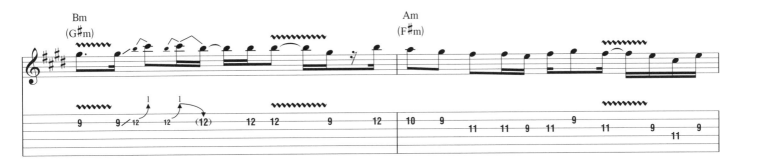

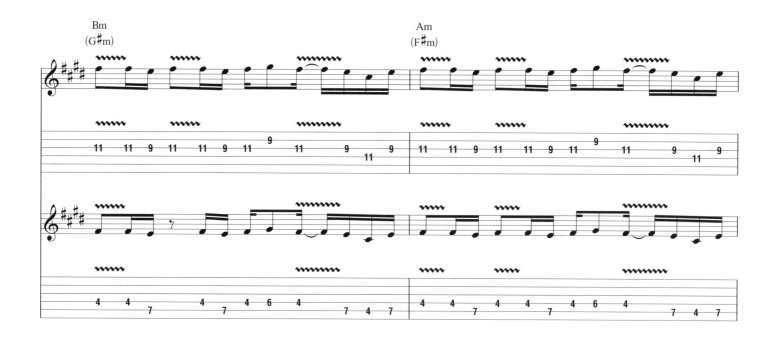

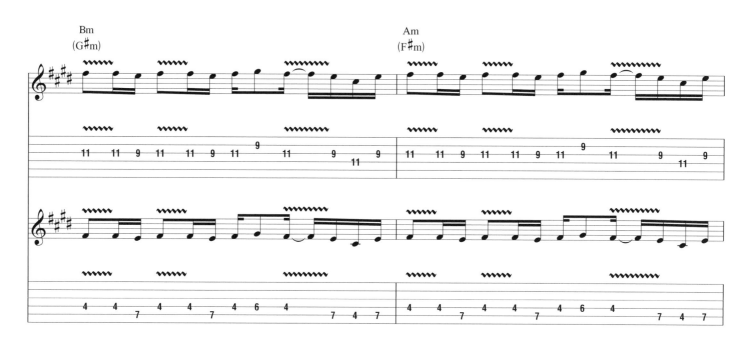

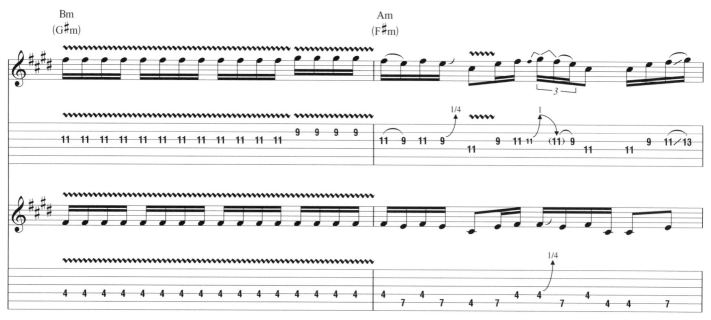

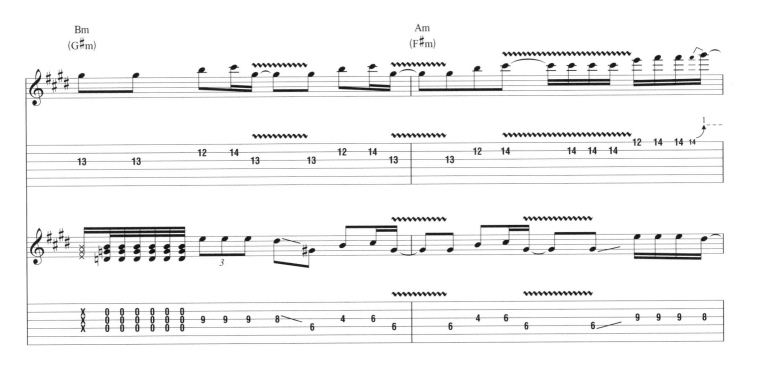

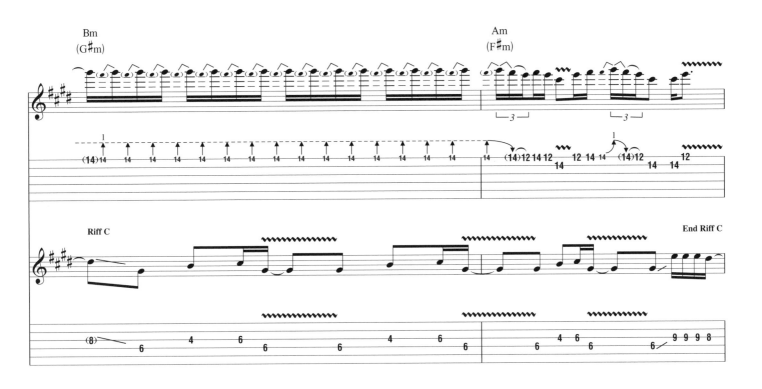

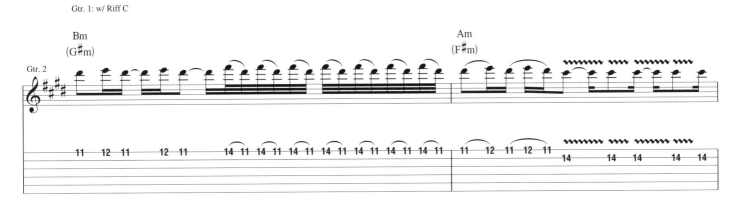

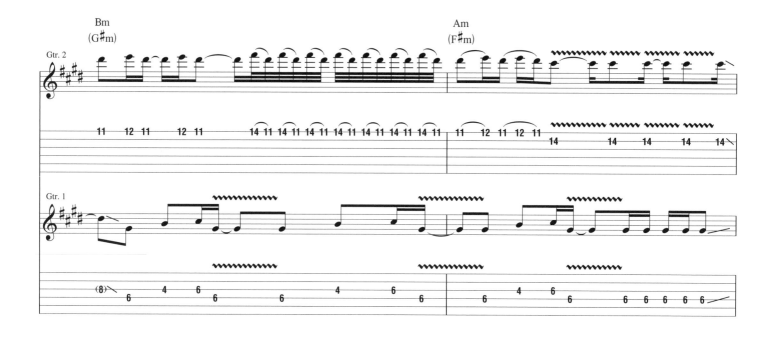

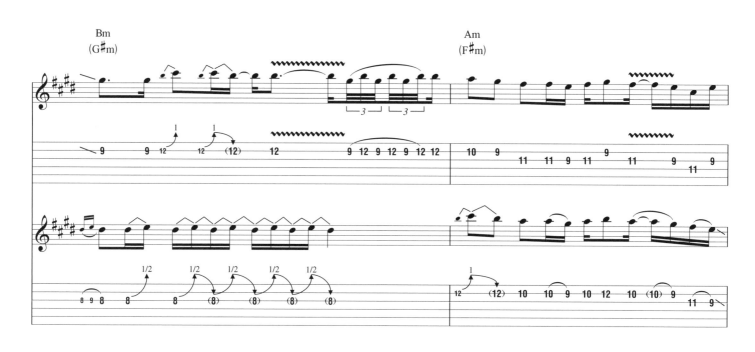

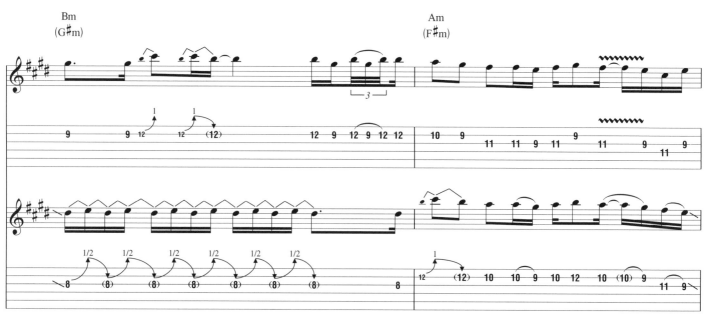

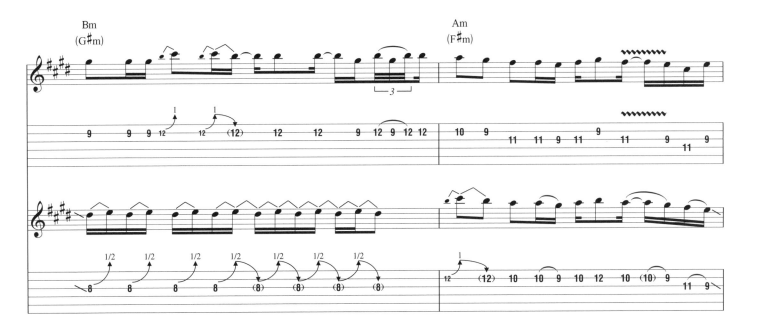

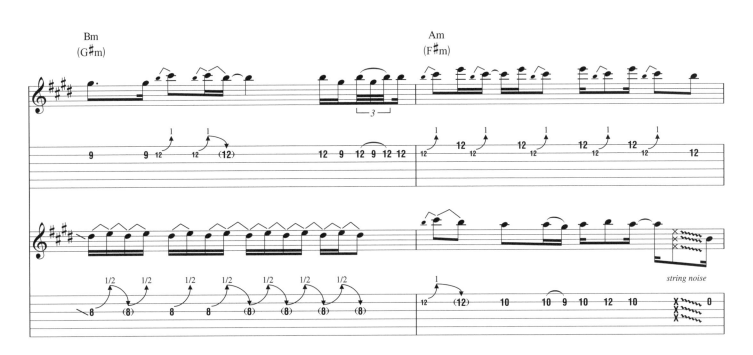

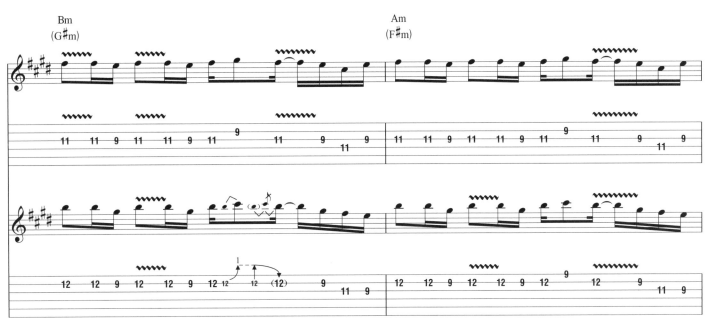

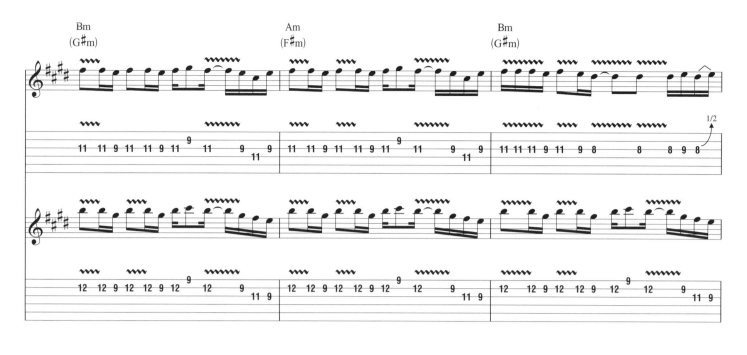

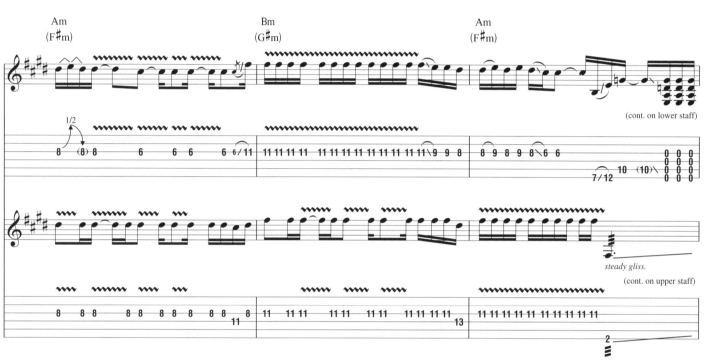

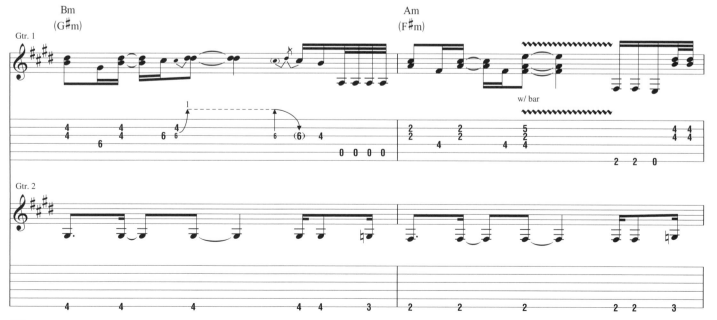

from *Evil Urges*

Look at You

Words and Music by Jim James

Gtr. 1: Capo III

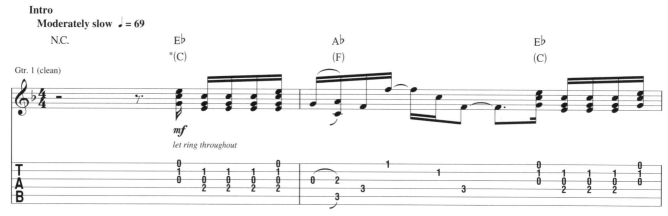

*Symbols in parentheses represent chord names respective to capoed guitar.
Symbols above represent actual sounding chords. Capoed fret is 0" in tab.
Chord symbols reflect overall harmony.

Off the Record

Words and Music by Jim James

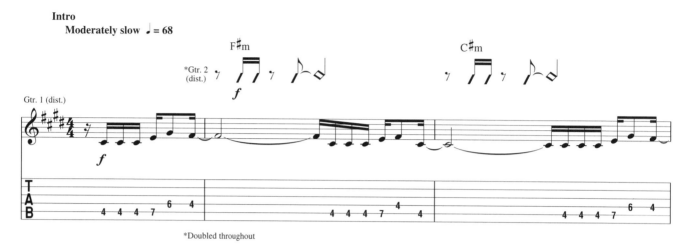

Intro

Moderately slow ♩ = 68

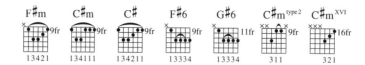

*Doubled throughout

Verse

Chorus

right, right, right, right. You've got to want to re - ar - range and keep it

off the rec - ord, off the rec - ord. You've got to know that we will change and keep it

Interlude

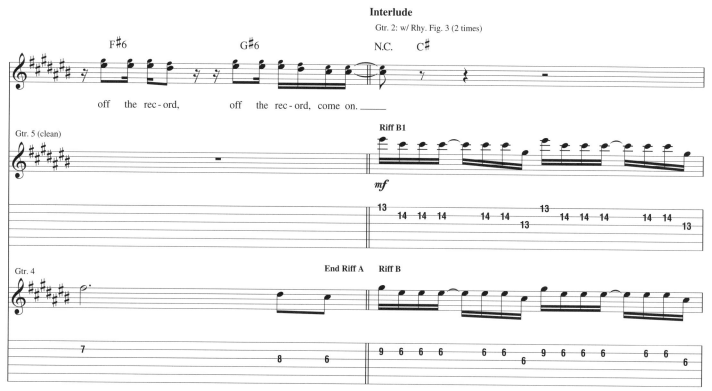

off the rec - ord, off the rec - ord, come on.

Pre-Chorus

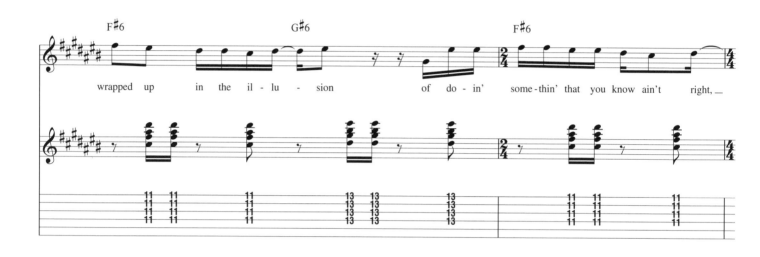

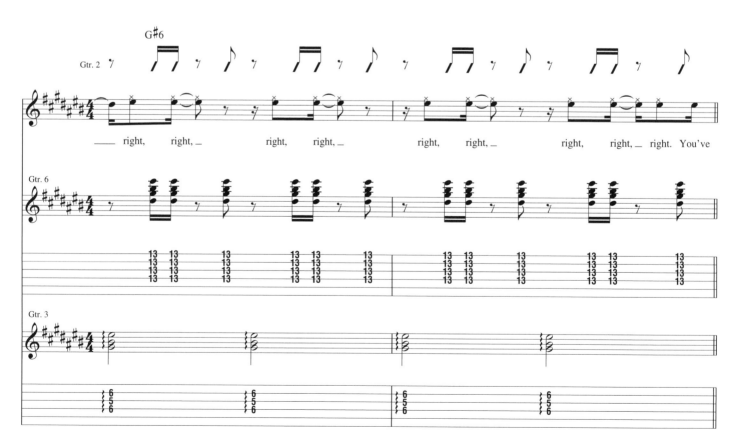

Chorus

Gtr. 2: w/ Rhy. Fig. 3 (4 times)
Gtr. 3 tacet
Gtr. 4: w/ Riff A

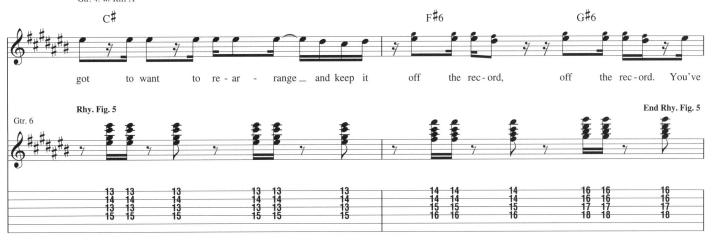

got to want to re - ar - range __ and keep it off the rec - ord, off the rec - ord. You've

Gtr. 6   **Rhy. Fig. 5**   **End Rhy. Fig. 5**

Gtr. 6: w/ Rhy. Fig. 5

got to know that we will change __ and keep it off the rec - ord, off the rec - ord. You've

Gtrs. 4 & 5: w/ Riffs B & B1

got to want to re - ar - range __ and keep it off the rec - ord, off the rec - ord. You've

got to know that we will change __ and keep it off the rec - ord, off the rec - ord, come on. __

Outro

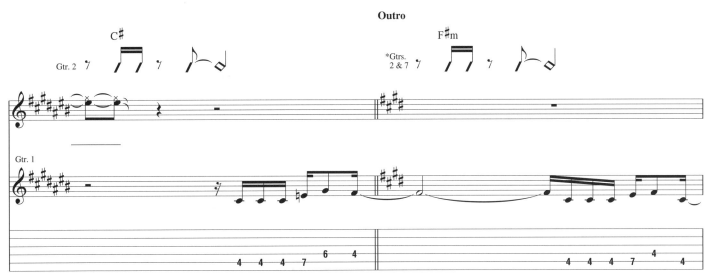

Gtr. 2

*Gtrs. 2 & 7

Gtr. 1

*Gtr. 7 (dist.), played *f*.

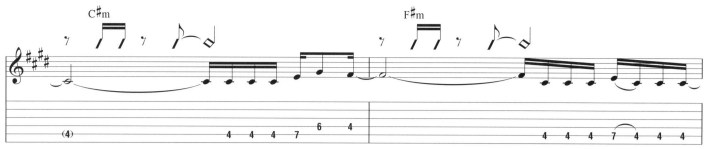

*Set for eighth-note triplet regeneration w/ 5 repeats.

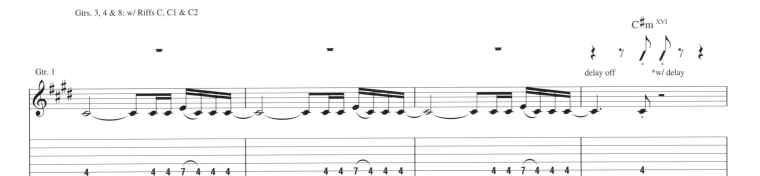

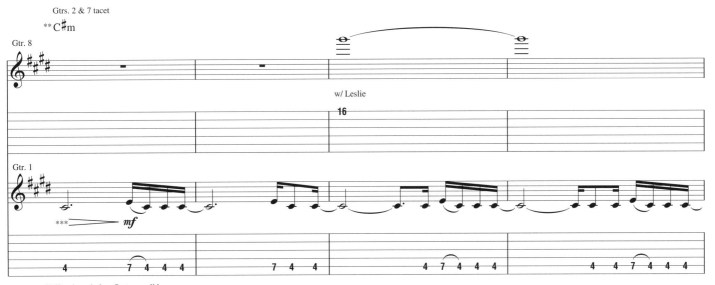

**Chord symbols reflect overall harmony.

***Roll back pre-distortion signal using a volume pedal.

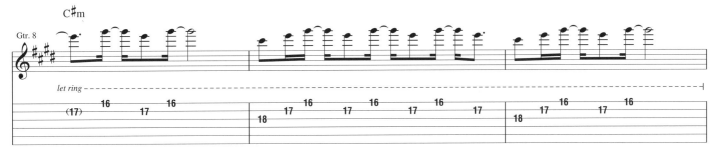

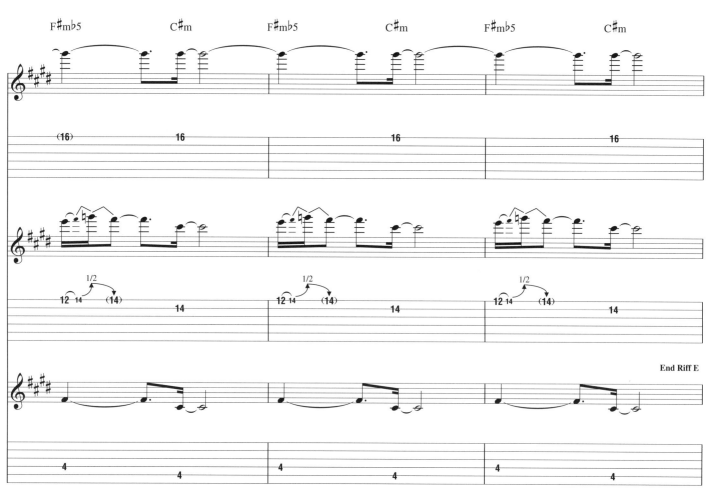

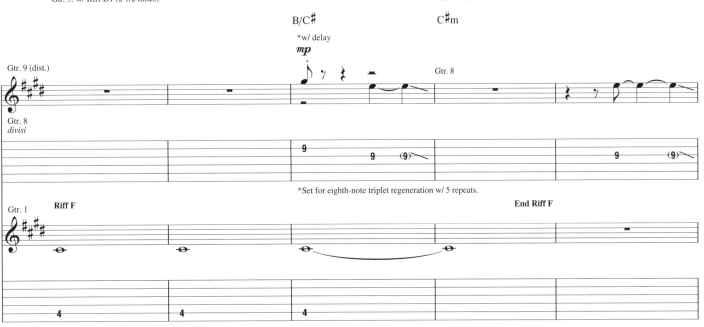

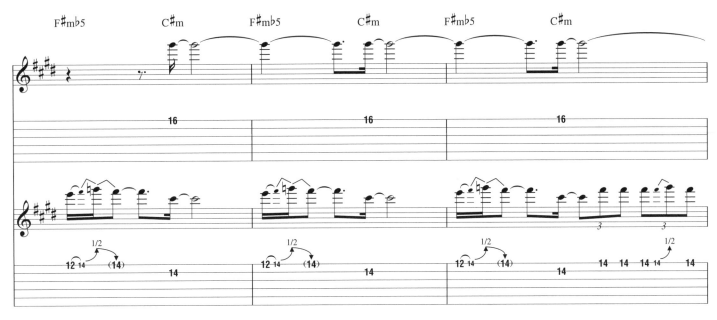

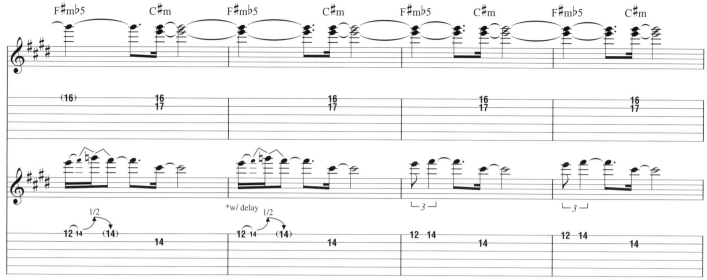

*Set for eighth-note triplet regeneration w/ 5 repeats.

Gtr. 3: w/ Riff D1 (2 times)
Gtr. 8 tacet

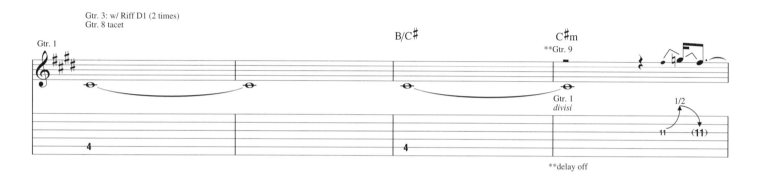

**delay off

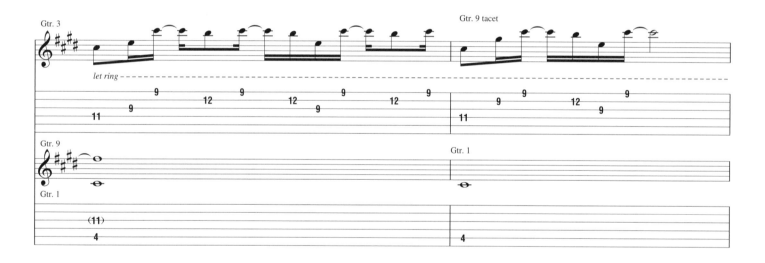

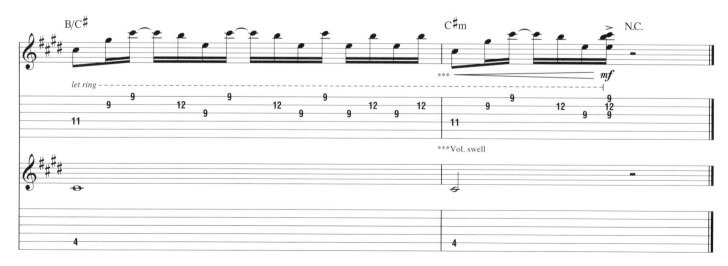

One Big Holiday

Words and Music by Jim James

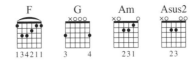

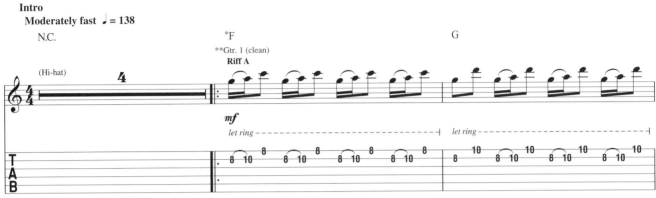

*Chord symbols reflect overall harmony.
**Two gtrs. arr. for one.

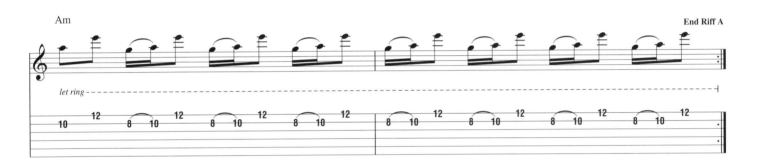

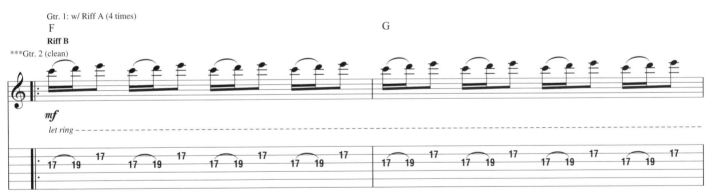

***Two gtrs. arr. for one.

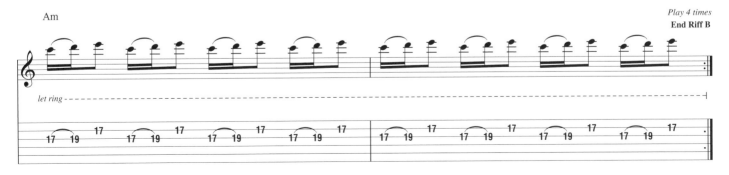

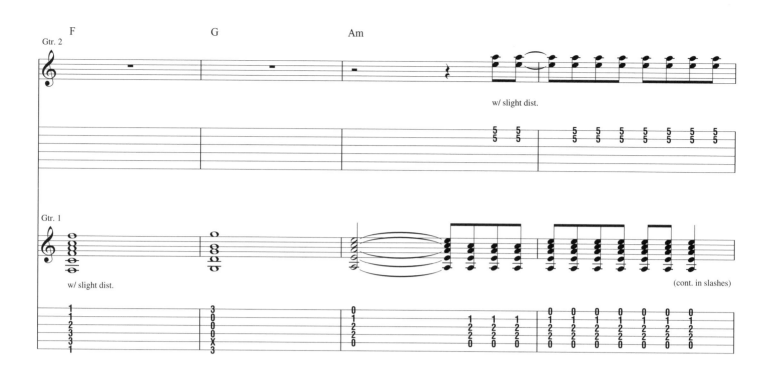

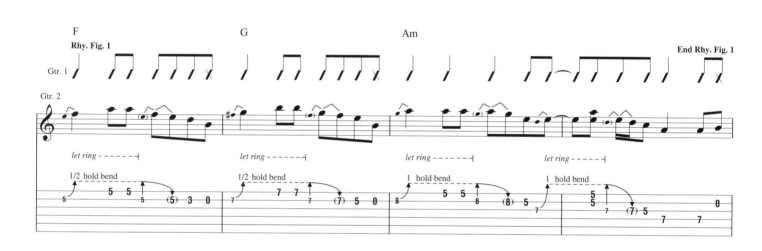

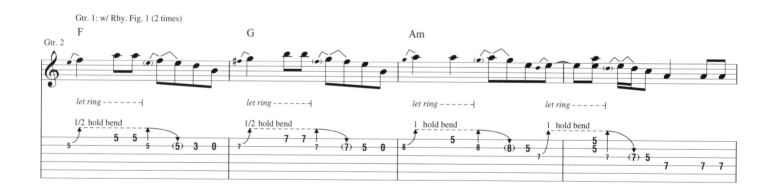

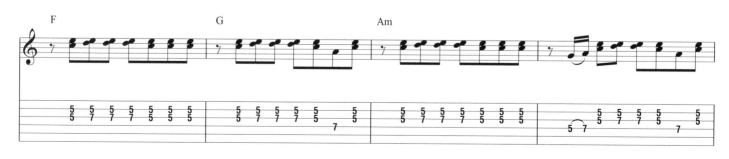

104

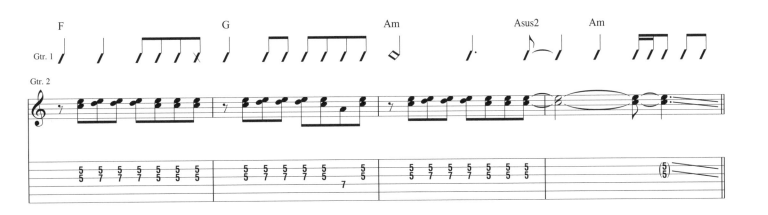

*Composite arrangement

*Bass plays C.

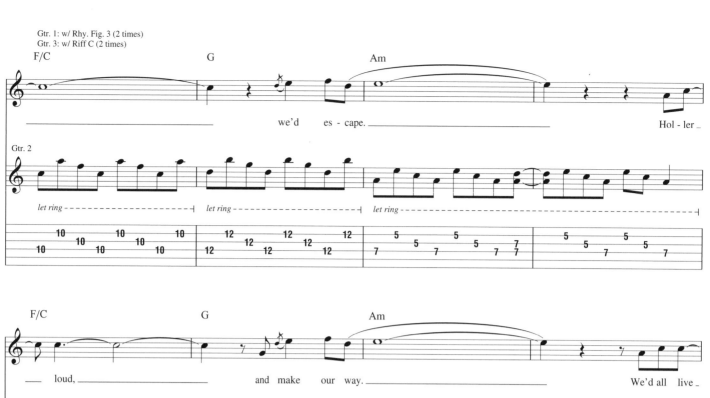

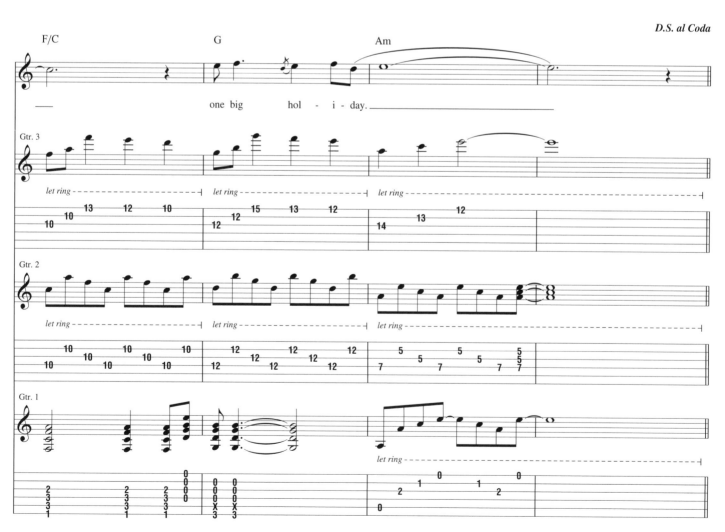

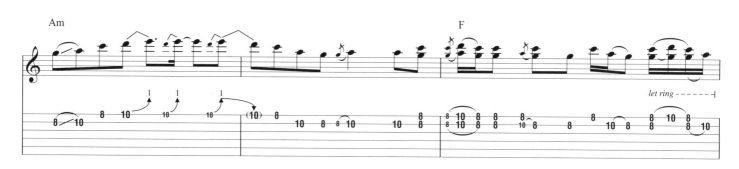

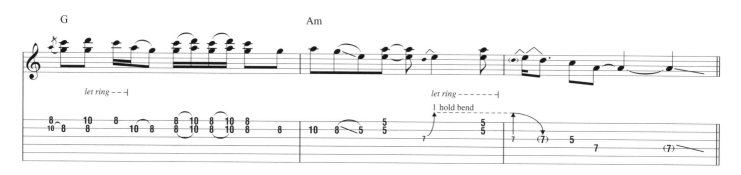

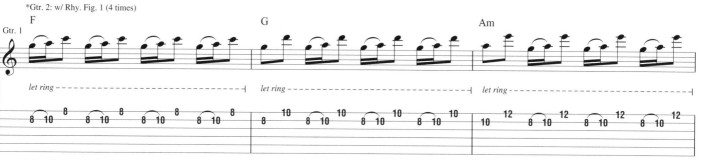

Guitar Solo

*Gtr. 2: w/ Rhy. Fig. 1 (4 times)

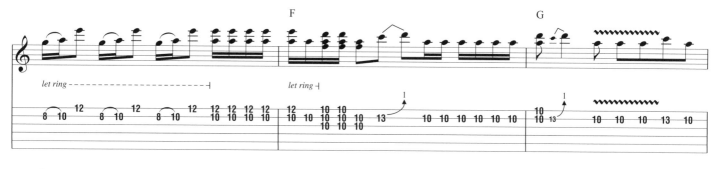

*dist. off, played *mp*

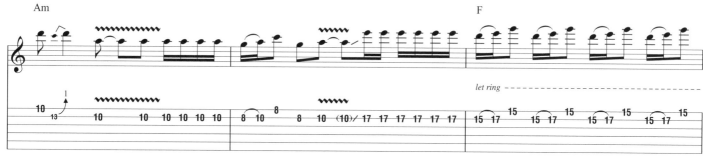

110

Smokin' from Shootin'

Words and Music by Jim James

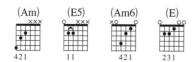

(Am) (E5) (Am6) (E)

Gtrs. 1 & 2: Capo I

Intro
Moderately fast ♩ = 136

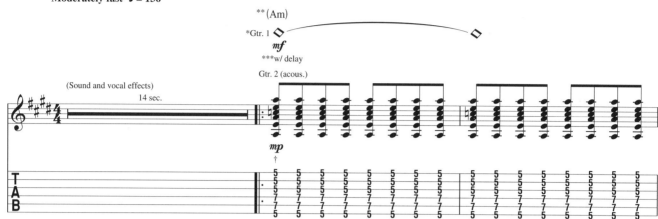

*Rhodes elec. piano arr. for gtr.
**Symbols in parentheses represent chord names respective to capoed guitar. Capoed fret is "0" in tab.
***Set for eighth-note regeneration w/ multiple repeats.
†Sound chords by slapping strings over 12th fret (next 8 meas.).

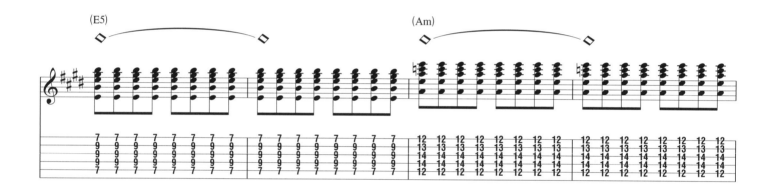

Verse
Gtr. 2 tacet
F5
††(E5)

(cont. in notation)

1. Have you had e - nough ___ ex - cite - ment now? ___ More

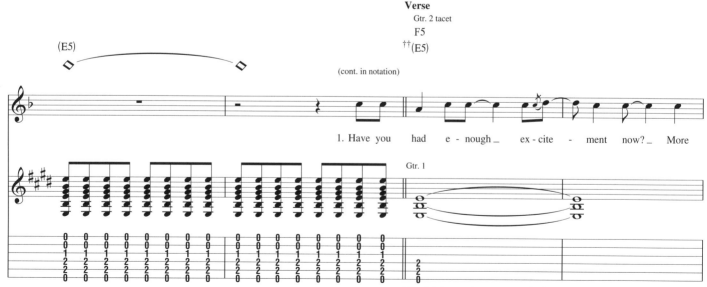

††Symbols in parentheses represent chord names respective to capoed guitar.
Symbols above represent actual sounding chords.

Interlude

F5
(E5)

Verse

Gtr. 1: w/ Rhy. Fig. 1 (2 times)

F5
(E5)   Am
                                                              (G♯m)

2. Who then was your sav - ior? Who then was your friend? ___

B♭
(A)   C
                                                                (B)

Who is now ___ com - mit - ted to the pres - ent? Is it some - one that ex - ists? ___

F5
(E5)   Am
                                                              (G♯m)

___ What is life ___ in God? ___ A per - fect vi - sion of ___ the self? ___

B♭
(A)

___ I al - ways thought we was a deal - in' with the one thing, now we are deal - ing with

C
(B)

Interlude
Half-time feel

(E5)
Rhy. Fig. 2
Gtr. 1

some - thing else, ___ oh. ___

Gtr. 2

Rhy. Fig. 2A

114

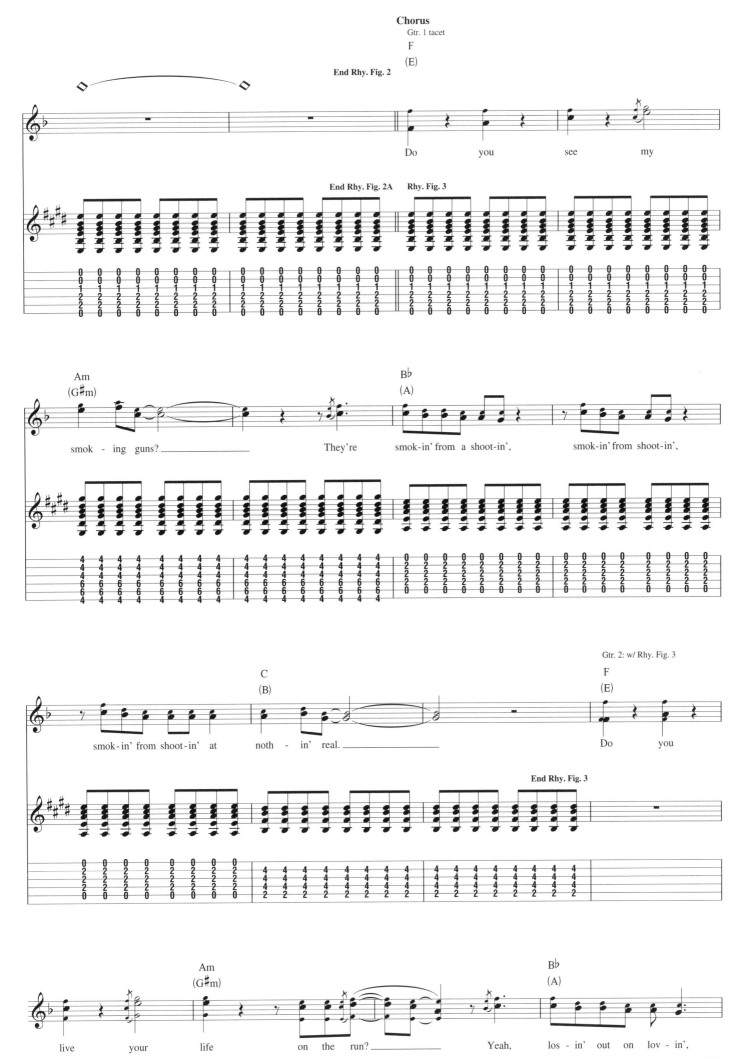

ask - in' for noth - in', run - nin' from some-thin' that is - n't there, _____ oh. _____

Gtr. 1

Interlude

Gtr. 2: w/ Rhy. Fig. 2A

Verse

Gtr. 1: w/ Rhy. Fig. 1 (2 times)
Gtr. 2: w/ Rhy. Fig. 3 (2 times)

3. Who makes my ___ de - ci - sions? Who reads all ___ your thoughts? ___

Gtr. 3 (elec.)

w/ dist.

What makes us ___ how we are? ___ Faith can't prove ___ what sci - ence ___ won't re - solve. ___

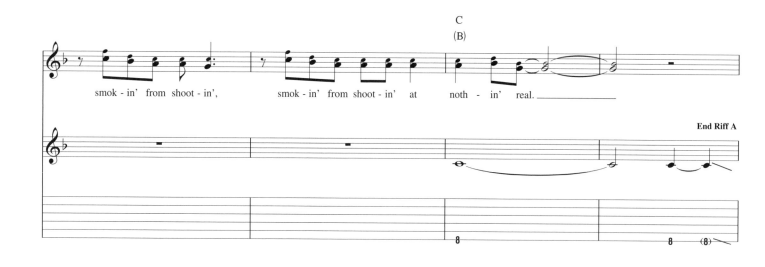

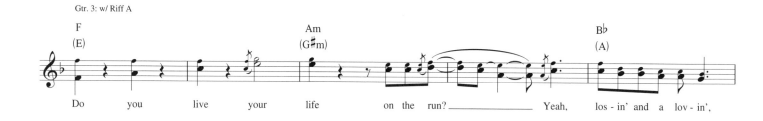

Interlude

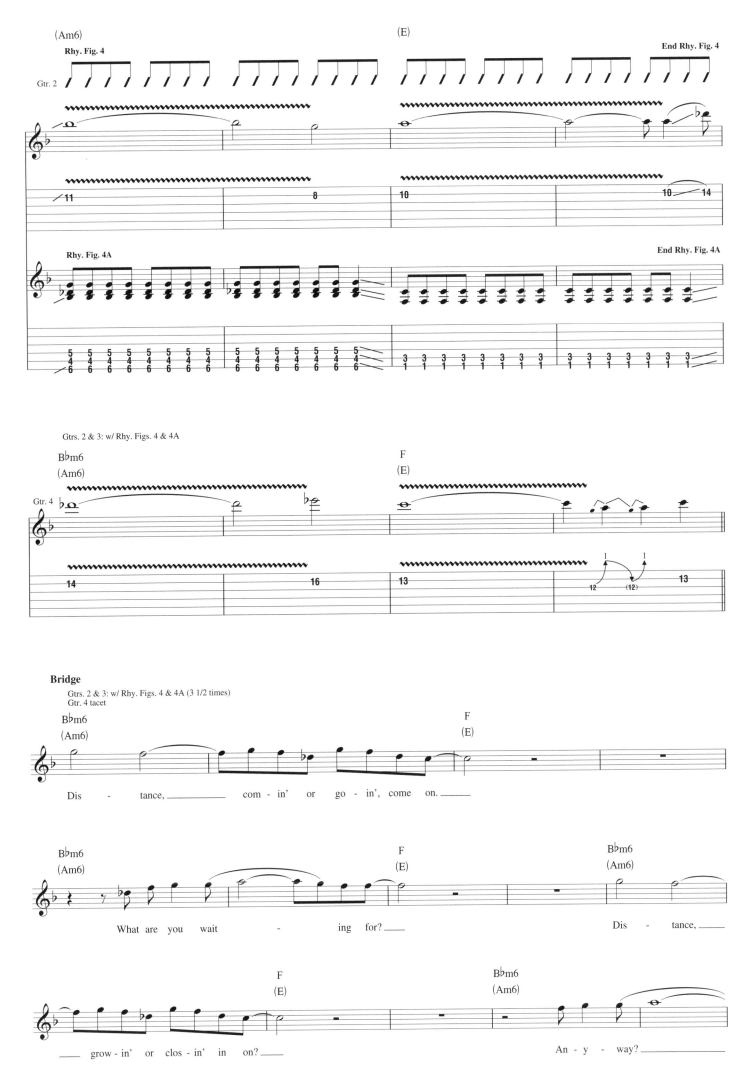

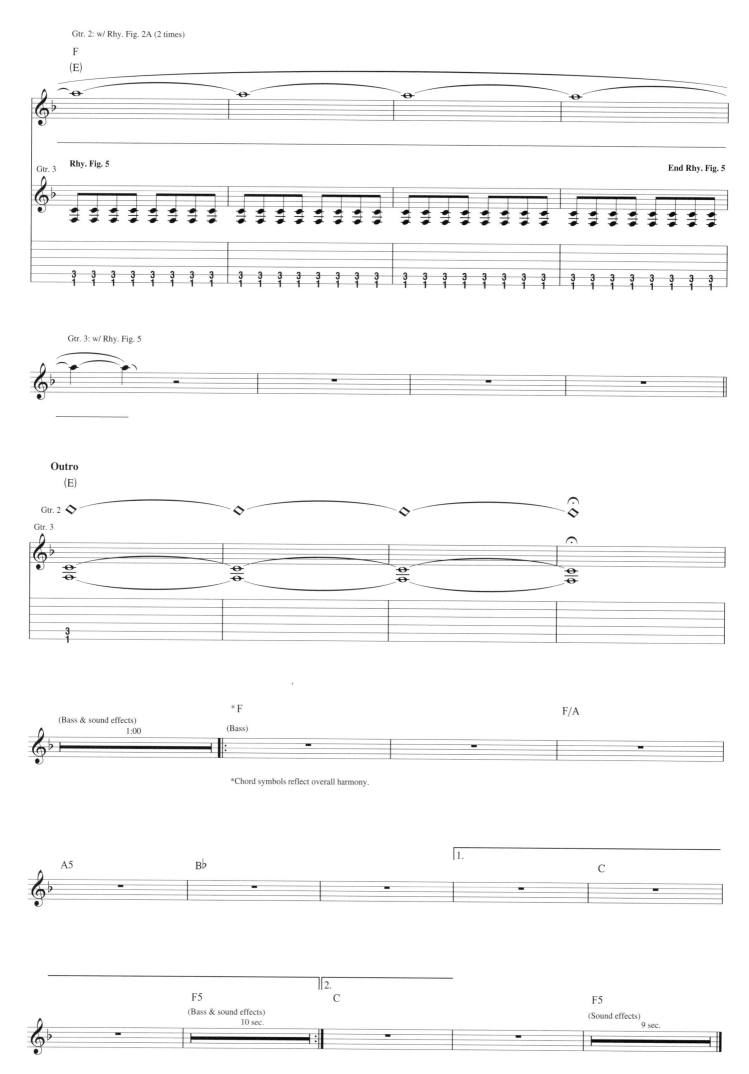

from *Evil Urges*

Thank You Too

Words and Music by Jim James

Gtrs. 1 & 2: Capo II

Intro
Slowly ♩ = 74

*Symbols in parentheses represent chord names respective to capoed guitar.
Symbols above represent actual sounding chords. Capoed fret is "0" in tab.
Chord symbols reflect overall harmony.

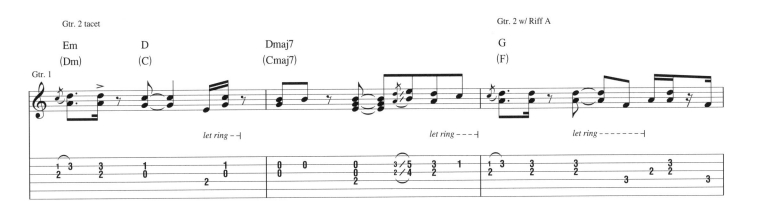

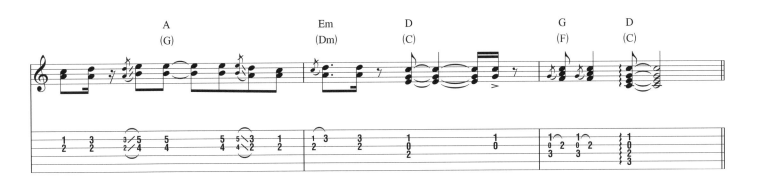

saw my na-ked heart. ___ You real-ly brought out the "na-ked" part. ___

___ I don't know what you were do-in'. I know I just want to thank you for think-

Chorus

in' of me. ___ I want to take you ___ for

*delay off

123

all that you are   al - though our   worlds _____ seem _____   far a - part. _____ I want to

see   you _____   through all that you do.   I want to   thank _____ you. _____

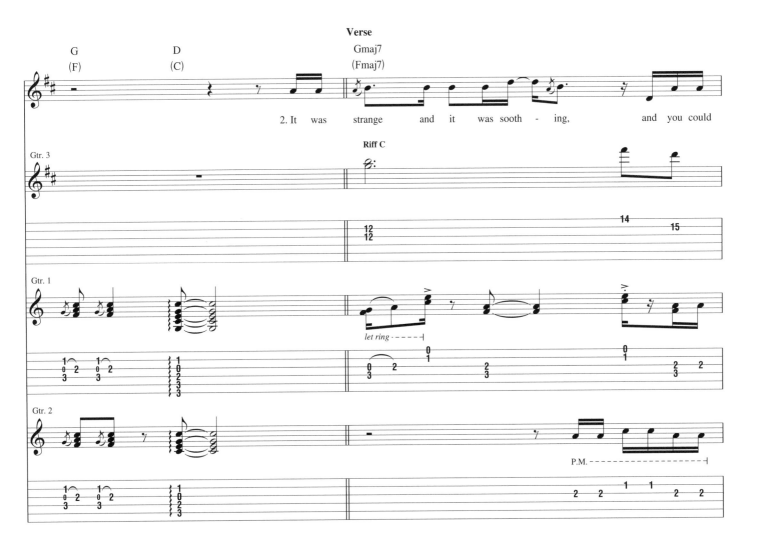

Gtr. 3: w/ Riff C

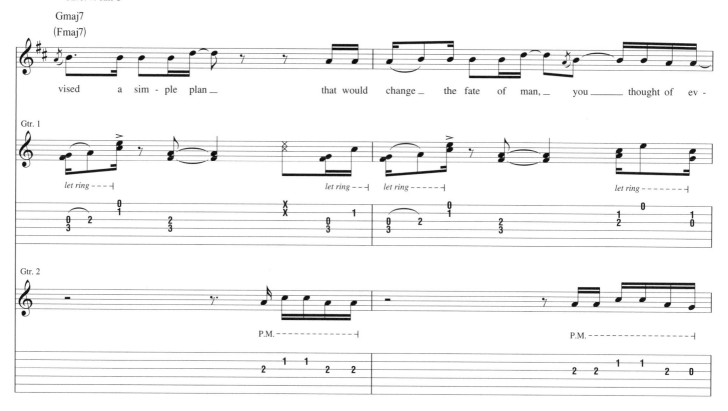

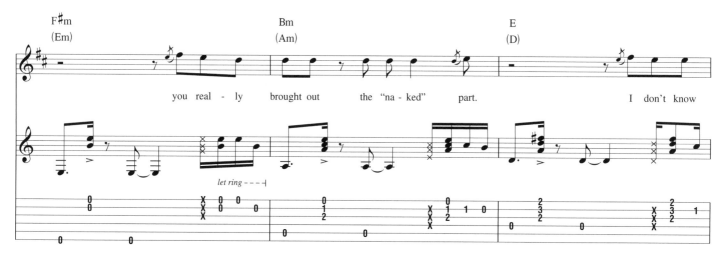

*T = Thumb on 6th string

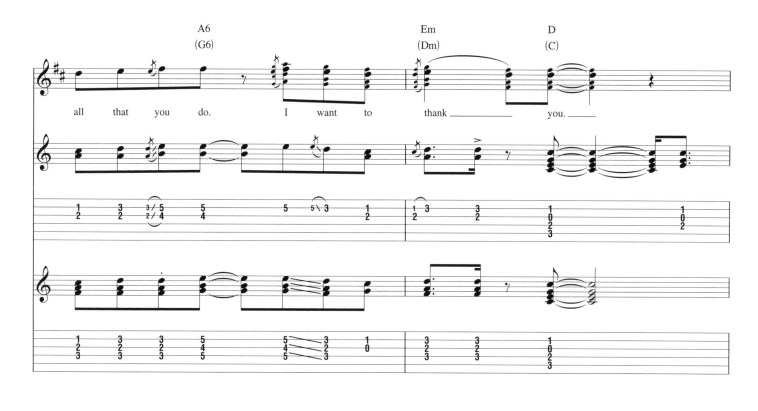

all that you do. I want to thank you.

Guitar Solo

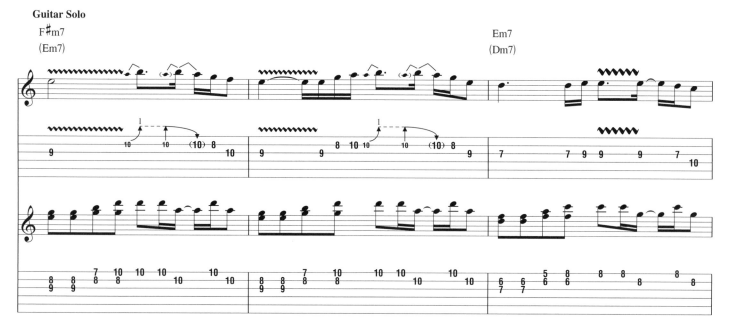

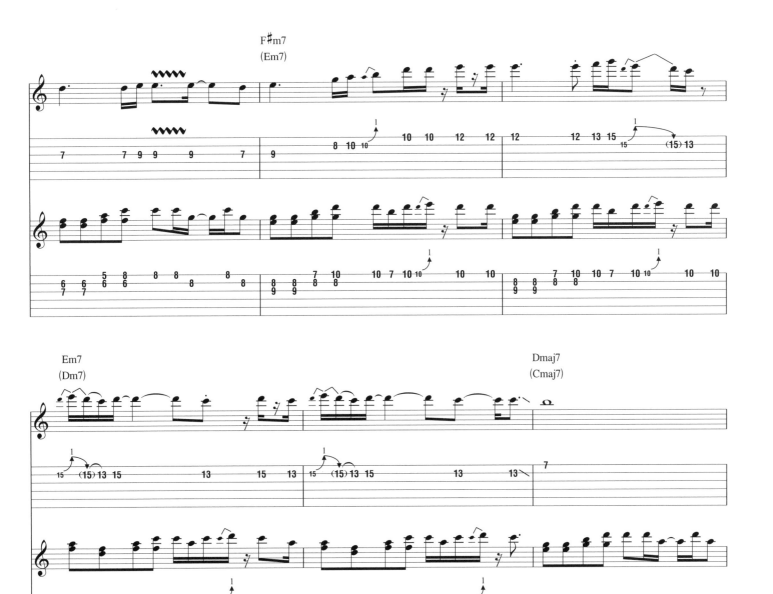

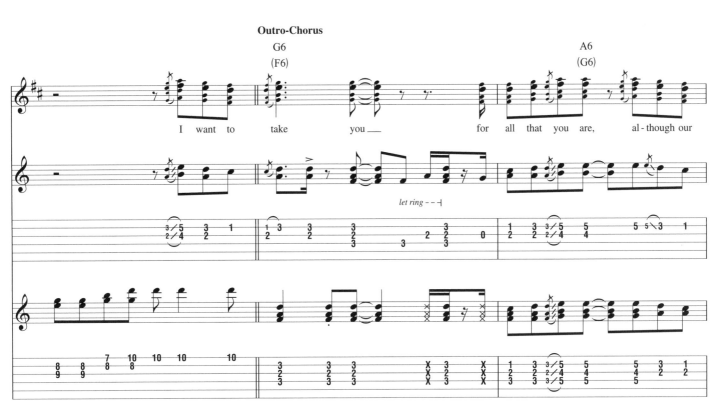

I want to take you ___ for all that you are, al-though our

let ring - - -

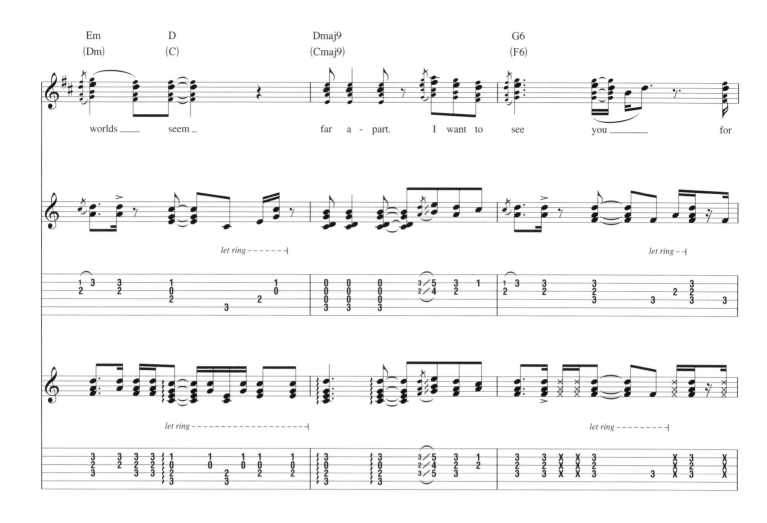

Ah.

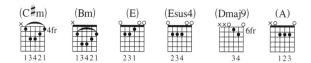

from *At Dawn*
The Way That He Sings

Words and Music by Jim James

Verse

1. Why's _____ it so strange _____ when they say _____ that the world's _____ mov-in' up-

Riff C

- wards? _____

End Riff C

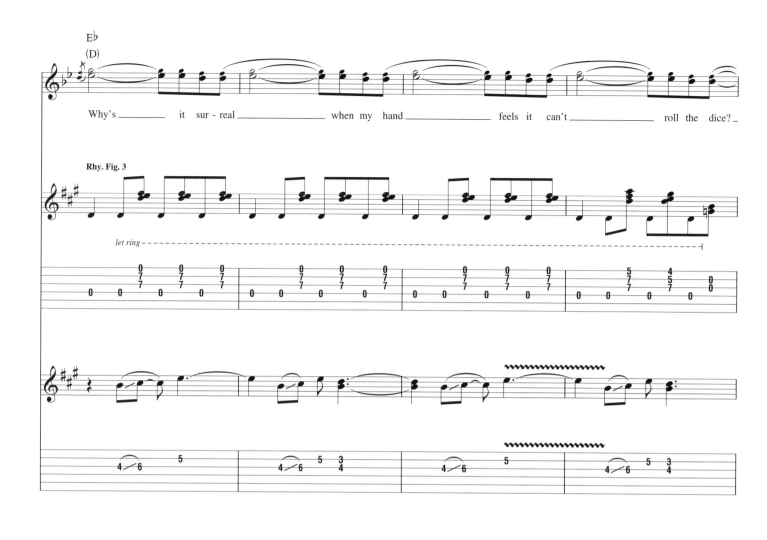

Why's _____ it sur-real _____ when my hand _____ feels it can't _____ roll the dice? _____

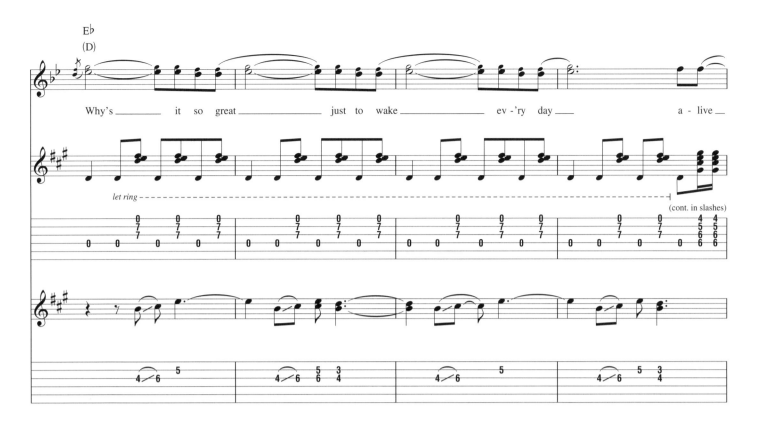

Why's _____ it so great _____ just to wake _____ ev -'ry day _____ a - live _____

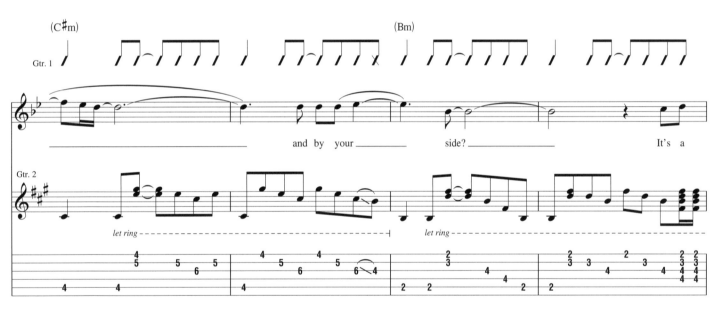

and by your _____ side? _____ It's a

mys - t'ry I guess, _____ there's lots of things _____ that I _____ can't _____ find. _____

It's not the
way ___ that you look, ___ but your move ___ that catch-es my ___ eye. ___

Interlude
Gtr. 1: w/ Rhy. Fig. 1 (2 times)
Gtr. 2: w/ Riff A (2 times)

Ah, ee, dom, dom. ___ Ah, ee, dom, dom, ___ dom, ah, ee, dom, dom. ___ Ah,

Why're _____ we so loud _____ when we say _____ it won't hap - pen _____ to us? _

Why _____ does my mind _____ blow to bits _____ ev - 'ry time _____ they play _

with this soul, ___ it's a mean-ing that ___ I un - der - stand. __ Ah,

Outro

Gtr. 1: w/ Rhy. Fig. 1 (4 times)
Gtr. 2: w/ Riff A (4 times)
Gtr. 4 tacet

ee, dom, dom, _ dom, ah, ee, dom, dom. _ Ah, ee, dom, dom, _ dom, ah, ee, dom, dom. _ Ah,

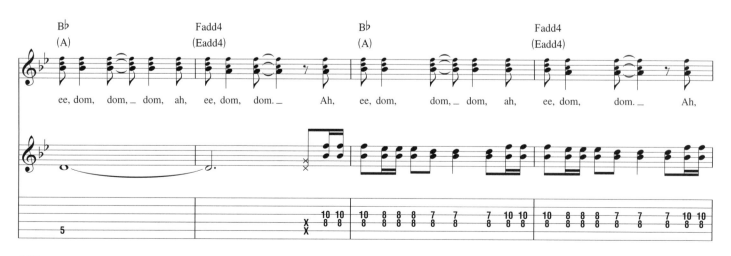

ee, dom, dom, _ dom, ah, ee, dom, dom. _ Ah, ee, dom, dom, _ dom, ah, ee, dom, dom. _ Ah,

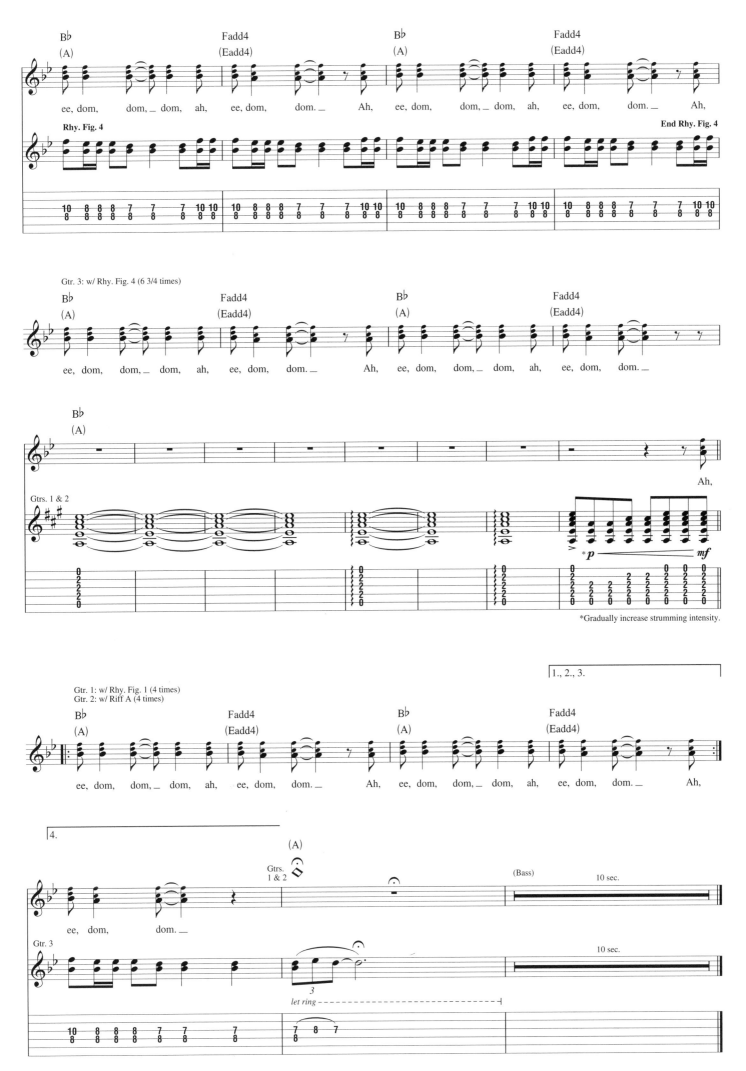

Guitar Notation Legend

Guitar music can be notated three different ways: on a *musical staff*, in *tablature*, and in *rhythm slashes*.

RHYTHM SLASHES are written above the staff. Strum chords in the rhythm indicated. Use the chord diagrams found at the top of the first page of the transcription for the appropriate chord voicings. Round noteheads indicate single notes.

THE MUSICAL STAFF shows pitches and rhythms and is divided by bar lines into measures. Pitches are named after the first seven letters of the alphabet.

TABLATURE graphically represents the guitar fingerboard. Each horizontal line represents a string, and each number represents a fret.

HALF-STEP BEND: Strike the note and bend up 1/2 step.

WHOLE-STEP BEND: Strike the note and bend up one step.

GRACE NOTE BEND: Strike the note and immediately bend up as indicated.

SLIGHT (MICROTONE) BEND: Strike the note and bend up 1/4 step.

BEND AND RELEASE: Strike the note and bend up as indicated, then release back to the original note. Only the first note is struck.

PRE-BEND: Bend the note as indicated, then strike it.

VIBRATO: The string is vibrated by rapidly bending and releasing the note with the fretting hand.

WIDE VIBRATO: The pitch is varied to a greater degree by vibrating with the fretting hand.

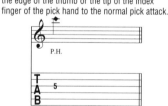

HAMMER-ON: Strike the first (lower) note with one finger, then sound the higher note (on the same string) with another finger by fretting it without picking.

PULL-OFF: Place both fingers on the notes to be sounded. Strike the first note and without picking, pull the finger off to sound the second (lower) note.

LEGATO SLIDE: Strike the first note and then slide the same fret-hand finger up or down to the second note. The second note is not struck.

SHIFT SLIDE: Same as legato slide, except the second note is struck.

TRILL: Very rapidly alternate between the notes indicated by continuously hammering on and pulling off.

TAPPING: Hammer ("tap") the fret indicated with the pick-hand index or middle finger and pull off to the note fretted by the fret hand.

NATURAL HARMONIC: Strike the note while the fret-hand lightly touches the string directly over the fret indicated.

PINCH HARMONIC: The note is fretted normally and a harmonic is produced by adding the edge of the thumb or the tip of the index finger of the pick hand to the normal pick attack.

PICK SCRAPE: The edge of the pick is rubbed down (or up) the string, producing a scratchy sound.

MUFFLED STRINGS: A percussive sound is produced by laying the fret hand across the string(s) without depressing, and striking them with the pick hand.

PALM MUTING: The note is partially muted by the pick hand lightly touching the string(s) just before the bridge.

RAKE: Drag the pick across the strings indicated with a single motion.

TREMOLO PICKING: The note is picked as rapidly and continuously as possible.

VIBRATO BAR DIVE AND RETURN: The pitch of the note or chord is dropped a specified number of steps (in rhythm), then returned to the original pitch.

VIBRATO BAR SCOOP: Depress the bar just before striking the note, then quickly release the bar.

VIBRATO BAR DIP: Strike the note and then immediately drop a specified number of steps, then release back to the original pitch.